KENNETH D. LAWRENCE
1520 Carter Lane, Woodbridge, VA 22191

D1781811

Introduction to Treasure Hunting

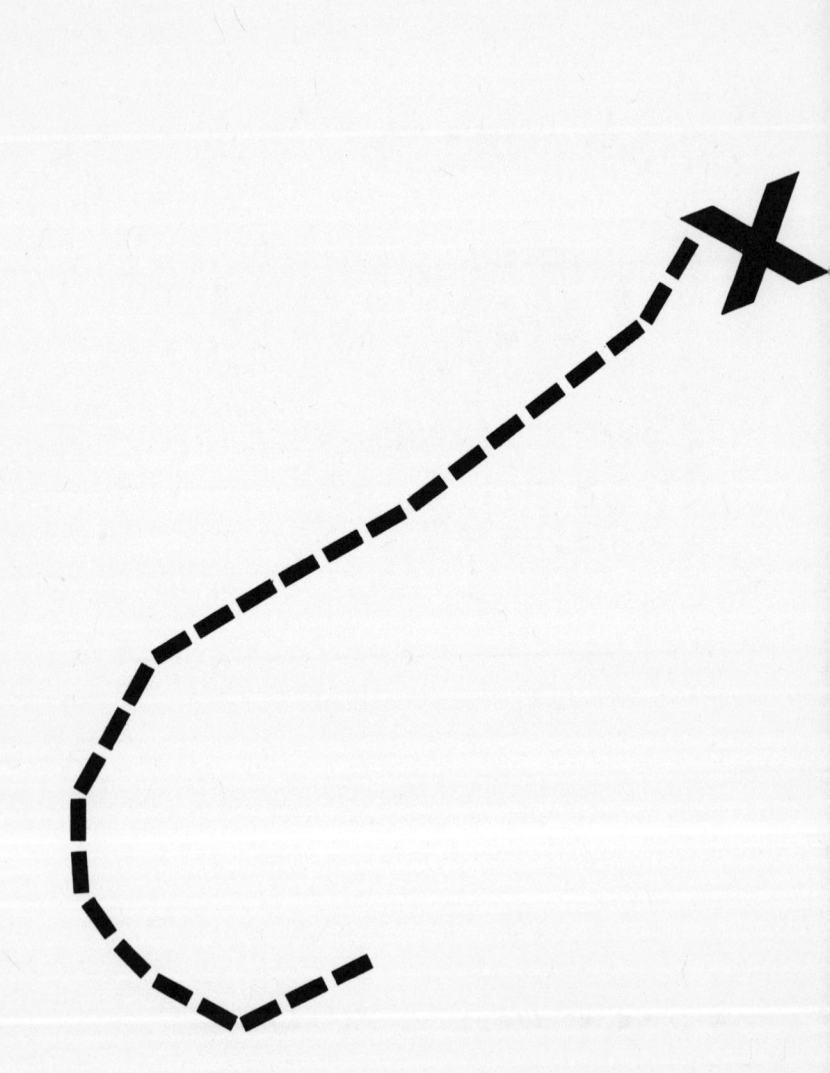

Introduction to Treasure Hunting

Alan Smith

STACKPOLE BOOKS

INTRODUCTION TO TREASURE HUNTING
Copyright © 1971 by
THE STACKPOLE COMPANY

Published by
STACKPOLE BOOKS
Cameron and Kelker Streets
Harrisburg, Pa. 17105

All rights reserved, including the right to reproduce this book or portions thereof in any form or by any means, electronic or mechanical, including photocopying, recording, or by any information storage and retrieval system, without permission in writing from the publisher. All inquiries should be addressed to Stackpole Books, Cameron and Kelker Streets, Harrisburg, Pennsylvania 17105.

Dedicated to my wife, Mary Lois,
for her tireless work at the typewriter
even unto the tenth revision

ISBN 0-8117-0924-8
Library of Congress Catalog Card Number 78-140743

Printed in U.S.A.

Contents

Treasure Map of the West   8

Treasure Map of the East   9

Acknowledgments   10

Introduction   11

1. The Hobby That Makes Adventure Profitable   13
Buried treasure that can be found in any neighborhood—How to make money while contributing to science and museums—Building collections of rare coins and battle relics—Starting a personal lost-and-found service—Recovering lost items for insurance companies

2. Buried Treasures from a Colorful Past   22
Sleuthing in old local newspapers on microfilm—Getting clues from historical society collections, history books, biographies, and diaries—How to use topographical maps of the U.S. Geological Survey—Finding abandoned townsites from atlases—Leads from local Indian history—Hidden silver treasure of the Shawnee Indians—Treasure-hunting success stories—Ghost towns and abandoned fort sites—Investigating the pioneer trails—Outlaws' money caches—Bernarr MacFadden's underground "bank" deposits—Posthole banks—Searching farm dumps for Americana—Hidden battle treasures from the Civil War and other military operations

3. The Hidden Riches of American Beaches 45
Exploits of the seventeenth-century buccaneers—Buried pirate gold—Beaches where coins from shipwrecks are washed ashore in Massachusetts, Delaware, New Jersey, Washington, and Texas—The treasures of Padre Island—The unfound wealth on Oak Island

4. Relics and Gold from Lakes and Sea 58
Dramatic salvaging operations—The lost golden galleons of Spain—Spanish wrecks in Florida waters accessible to scuba divers and snorklers—Spanish shipments of mercury lost off Hispaniola—Ships sunk in the Great Lakes—Battle relics from the War of 1812 and the pre-Revolutionary Indian wars under Lake Erie

5. The Lowdown on Metal Detectors—Mystical and Electronic 71
The mysterious divining pendulum—How to test yourself for psychic treasure-finding ability—Electronic detectors: beat frequency, induction balance, transmitter-receiver, and proton magnetometer—Prices—The importance of quality—Bargains

6. How to Make Your Own Detector 91
Cost savings—Hand-wiring method—Etched circuit board method—Tools, supplies, electronic parts, and hardware—Field trials—Troubleshooting

7. Surefire Ways to Treasure-Hunting Success 115
Operating beat frequency detectors—Battery care—Learning to identify signals emitted by various objects—Effect of corrosion on detection depth of coins—When to use meters—Marking hot spots—Digging equipment, sifters, and containers—Gear for working in water—Staying comfortable—Safety precautions—Avoiding crowds

8. Finding, Cleaning, and Selling Coins 129
How deep coins are buried—Spectacular coin finds—Fairgrounds, playgrounds, parks, and other hot spots—Searching abandoned buildings—Removing soil, sand, and corrosion from coin faces—Grading system for coins—Mint marks—Guide to coin rarity—The disappearance of silver money and its effect on coin values

9. Modern-day Methods of Prospecting for the Hobbyist 145
How to identify possible meteorites—Where to find precious and semiprecious stones—How gold deposits were formed—Gold-bearing rivers and streams—Underwater prospecting for gold—Panning for gold—Lost Indian silver mines in Ohio and Michigan

10. Obligations of the Treasure Hunter 162
Getting permission to search private property—Returning property to owners—How to avoid litigation—The income tax—Removing treasure from sod and buildings without damage—Tipping off treasure hunters who follow you

Metal Detector Manufacturers 170

Electronic Parts Supply Houses 171

Publishers of Treasure-Hunting Periodicals 172

Recommended Reading 173

Sources of Information 181

Treasure Maps Legend 182

Index 186

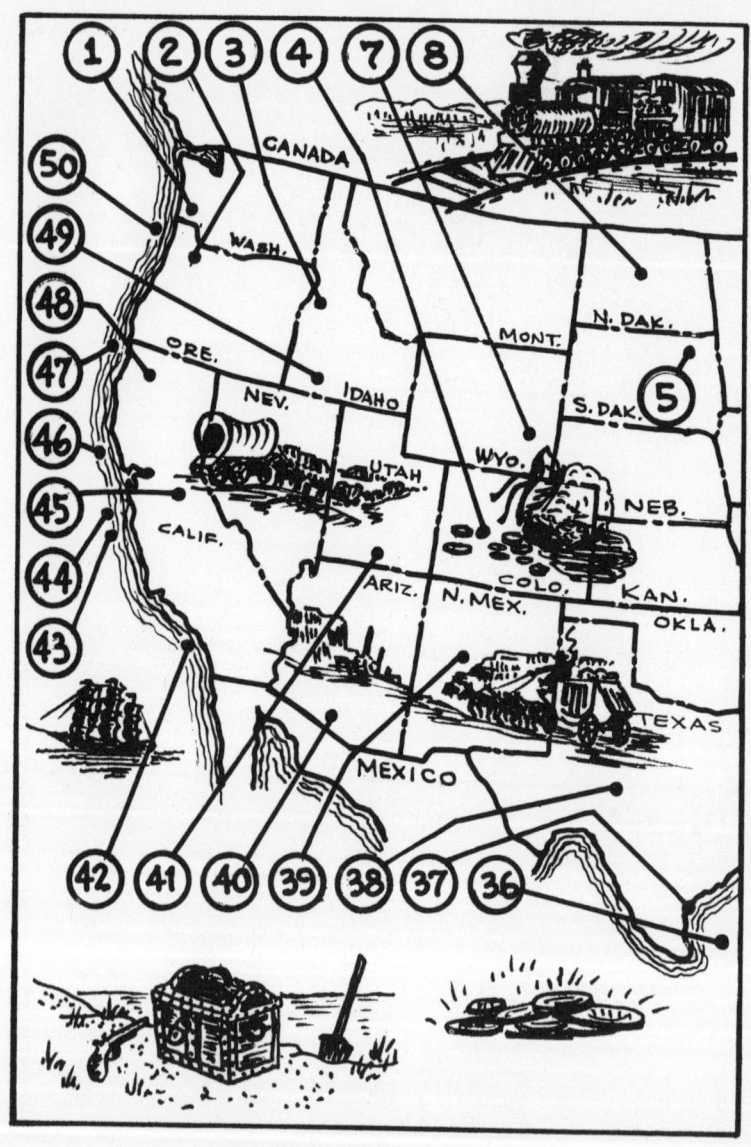

Treasure Map of the West

(See pp. 182-185 for Treasure Maps Legend.)

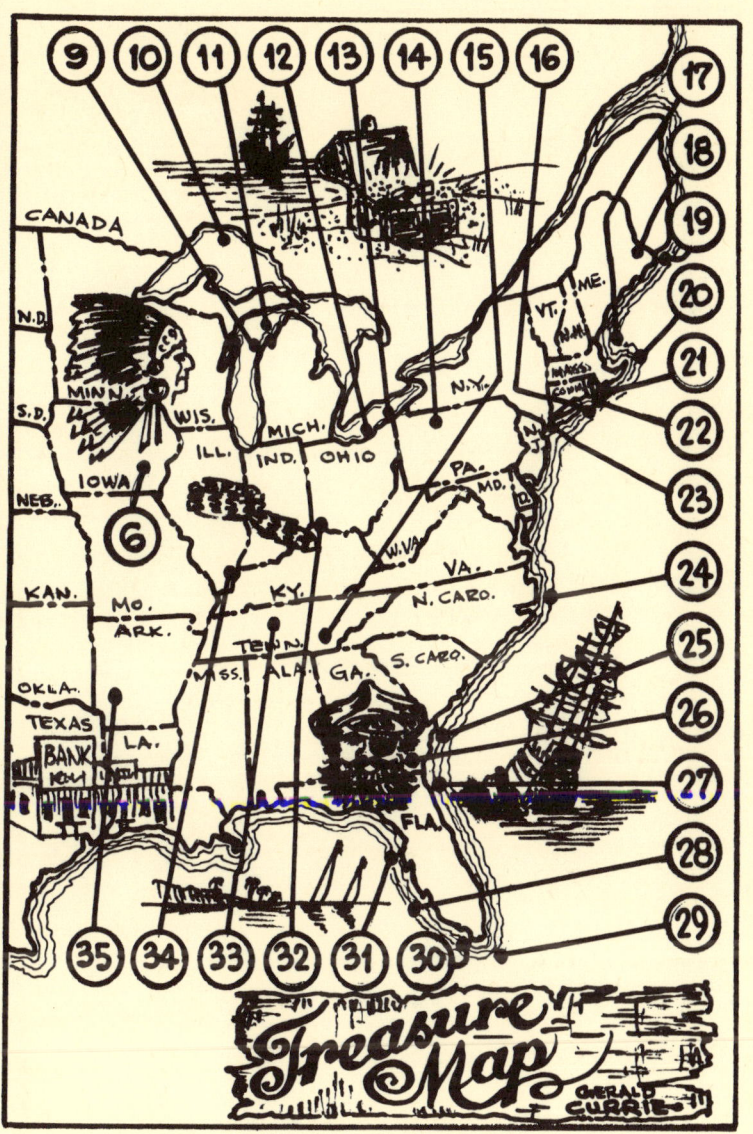

Treasure Map of the East

(See pp. 182-185 for Treasure Maps Legend.)

Acknowledgments

THIS book would not be complete without a fervent expression of gratitude for the willing hands which helped me to surmount the many hurdles along the way.

First a word of thanks to Gerald Currie and Martin Murphy for their art work. Next, to Donald Jankowski and to Glen Francisco, for the draftsmanship evident in maps and drawings, many thanks.

Special thanks to the Flint Public Library staff whose aid and interest helped to shorten the labor of research.

Thanks also, for the support and encouragement received from historical societies, state information offices, and other official state agencies, even though it was impossible to use in this book all the information which came in answer to our queries.

I also wish to thank Mr. Wesley Thomas for his care and assistance with the preparation of this book. And thanks to Gene Ballinger, manager of The Association, Oscoda, Michigan, for permission to reproduce the Search and Salvage Agreement on page 164 and for taking time out from a most pressing schedule to sit down for a talk about treasure hunting.

Introduction

HAVE you ever felt separated by a couple of light years from the fun and excitement of sudden wealth found in a rusty tin can, under a rotten log, or beneath the porch of a ruined house? And haven't you wished that you too could just once find something of more value than a three-cent deposit pop bottle, a cut-up golf ball, or a broken Boy Scout knife? Well, take heart. Wishing can become doing.

It's easy to join a select group of men and women of all ages who hunt successfully for treasure. This book tells how these searchers operate and what they are looking for.

Unlike people who accidentally find money caches, on-purpose treasure finders don't do much talking. The shortage of information and publicity about treasure hunting tends to keep newcomers out of this fabulous hobby. Our purpose is to let the beginner in on a few secrets and show him how to get started.

To begin the action, send postcards to some of the publishers of treasure-hunting periodicals listed in the back of this book. Ask them for sample copies of their publications. Some of them are free!

Next send a card to each of the metal detector manufacturers listed in the back of the book. Ask each one to send its sales brochure. The next step is to forget, for now, that gold hoard you have been thinking about that is buried a couple of thousand miles away somewhere across the country. Begin, instead, to think about the treasure that is literally under your nose. This book tells how to find it.

A pot of gold cannot be guaranteed at the end of every rainbow, but the exciting adventure of the hunt will be more than ample reward. And, with just a little luck, you might find a real pot of gold and not a rainbow in sight.

chapter one

The Hobby That Makes Adventure Profitable

TREASURE is where you find it. At least one large treasure cache probably exists within a fifty-mile radius of every community in the United States.

Obviously, larger communities will have more potential targets, but wherever people have gathered to play and work there are valuable things hidden close by. These treasures vary in size from a cluster of coins to be found around the first base bag on a sandlot ball diamond, to a genuine two-karat jewel diamond set in an engagement ring and lost at a local swimming beach. In between lies a spread of valuable items that for variety keeps the hunter constantly guessing about what will appear next. Tools, antique auto parts, rings, bracelets, jeweled tie clasps, knives, historic firearms, spent lead and steel bullets, cannon shot, coins, medals, and earrings, are just a few of the exciting finds commonly unearthed.

An elderly lady on the east coast who is an avid treasure

hunter makes a constant round of certain public parks that are within her reach during the summer months. On a regular schedule she passes the search loop of a metal detector over every inch of sand. Her treasure trove has varied from golf clubs to gold-plated cigarette lighters. And don't think for an instant that these items can't be counted as treasure.

Twelve-year-old Rusty Ayres of Midland, Michigan, used his father's homemade locator to find an expensive gold-filled cigarette lighter when the owner gave up after a day-long search at a local beach. The ten-dollar reward Rusty got for returning the lighter was the best kind of treasure—the kind that can be spent.

Of course, cash in the hand is definitely the most negotiable of all the valuables which can be obtained from a hiding place, but not necessarily the most thrilling. Would you think it exciting, for instance, to find a meteorite? These objects from outer space plummet to earth everywhere, and the genuine article can put hard cash in the pocket. Payment of five dollars a pound is not unusual and it can go even higher. Besides the financial reward, recovery and sale of a meteorite will serve science, and who can turn down an opportunity like that? A letter of thanks from a leading authority on meteorites would be a reward in itself. (See Chapter 9 for tips on identifying meteorites.)

The Value of Historical Relics

A well-preserved frontier pistol or a Civil War rifle can be more welcome and often brings a higher price than a like amount of silver. Many people hunting for treasure prefer to find important relics rather than some forms of precious metal. It depends to a great extent upon one's sense of history, or what sort of things a treasure hunter cares for the most—perhaps as a collector. And well-preserved relics are more easily converted to cash than are gold bars, for gold bars *must* be turned in to the Treasury Department.

The Hobby That Makes Adventure Profitable 15

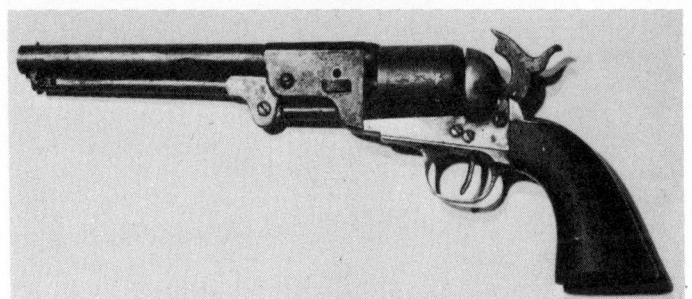

Civil War relic.—*Photo courtesy Kenneth White, Sr.*

This Gunnison .44 caliber Confederate revolver was found under the floor of a ramshackle house in North Carolina in August 1968 with the aid of an electronic metal detector. It is marked "C.S.A." and valued in excess of $700.

Treasure hunters enjoy the fascination of locating forgotten battlefields for their relics. There is hardly an occupied corner of the North American continent that at one time or another has not seen troops on the march or armies in battle—Indian war, Revolutionary War, and Civil War; east to west, north to south, it has been going on for at least three centuries. Inside the overall battle picture, no matter which war one chooses to study, small, intense action highlights are often well documented as to location. Such information may lead to a harvest of battle relics which may be sold to collectors or museums at a neat profit.

Somewhere under Ohio soil lie a quantity of historically valuable inscribed lead plates buried by an early French explorer to certify the right of France to a few million acres of the Ohio Valley. The engraving on each plate declared that all land to the north and all land to the west of that particular location was now claimed by France. History reveals, however, that the Frenchman made a futile though colorful attempt to get this area for his homeland. The explorer's name was Pierre Joseph Celeron. He entered the old Northwest by way of the Ohio River in 1749. For courage and digging holes

Spanish silver cross.—*Photo courtesy Kenneth White, Sr.*

This priceless treasure is one of a number of *Spanish* relics dated from 1690 to 1756 found with detectors in Arizona. It bears the name of Father Kino, Jesuit missionary explorer in the American Southwest.

along the way, he took along with him 235 well-equipped soldiers.

No one knows for certain just how many plates remain, but there were many of them at one time. Pierre Joseph buried a plate at the outlet of each major stream entering the Ohio River, and a couple of them have since then been reported as found by accident.

Celeron buried one of the plates only a few hours before it was hastily dug up again. It seems that a Seneca Indian happened to attend one of Celeron's ownership proclamation ceremonies. He listened politely to the speeches and watched the digging, all the while appearing awed and impressed by the ceremony. The instant, however, the coast was clear, he retrieved the plate and sent it by a special rider to a British friend of his by the name of Sir William Johnson. The Seneca Indians wanted the British to know of the Frenchman's activities. The report, however, was hardly needed, because Celeron himself made no secret of what was going on. If Pierre Joseph did as he intended, a lot of plates remain underground, and if somebody with a metal detector finds one or more of these plates, there is no telling how high some museum might bid to get possession of such a relic.

Searching for important tokens of the past may be more profitable than concentrating on lost money hoards. For one thing, relics are abundant. Secondly, there is steady enough demand to insure quick conversion to cash.

A trip or two to a local library and some friendly persuading of the older residents in an area will uncover many clues to the location of battlefields, forts, parade grounds, trading posts, stage stops, trails, military roads, and long-vanished pioneer villages. Many commonplace sites of yesteryear hide relics which, in addition to their cash value, provide a valuable link with the past and should be placed in public view.

Steve Herzog of Fort Gibson, Oklahoma has accumulated an extensive coin and relic collection by using a metal locator around old Fort Gibson. His finds include parts of military uniforms: buckles, buttons, and spurs. In addition, the telltale voice of his detector has led him to guns, melted silver, knives, and coins going all the way back to a 1775 Spanish one-real piece.

Such 200-year-old reals are, of course, impossible to get from circulation, but the soil of the old Northwest Territory contains coins as old and even older than 200 years. Unfortunately for all get-rich-quick schemes, though, the old Northwest Territory comprises a large area.

Coins

In the United States, at least, coins and other valuables have been accumulating underground at a fairly steady rate for a period of up to 400 years. The earth is a gigantic piggy bank just waiting to be cracked open.

A disciplined imagination will open this storehouse of treasure trove. Clues to rich finds don't drop out of the sky. They must be coaxed out with serious thinking. Fortunately, lost coins are not usually widely scattered; they occur in concentrations. To locate these concentrations, treasure hunters should first learn where in each locality people have regularly gathered over a long period of time. This especially includes those spots once popular, but no longer even thought of. Chapter 8 lists some of these places, and offers a guide to some outstanding coin values.

Starting a Lost-and-Found Service

Besides relics and coins, treasure hunters are constantly finding large quantities of rings and other jewelry. In fact, anyone with good metal-detecting equipment can operate a profitable personal lost-and-found service. People often pay sizeable rewards for the return of jewelry and other valuable items.

To get an idea of what it means, in money terms, to lose a ring, visit some jewelry stores. Do some window shopping and be sure to look at the expensive price tags.

Jewelers sell thousands of rings every year: wedding rings, engagement rings, fraternal order rings, signet rings, birthstone rings, and so on. Every year countless proud owners report loss of their rings, many of which can be recovered by scanning likely places with an electronic metal locator.

The Hobby That Makes Adventure Profitable 19

A few of the coins and rings found by the author in spare-time hunting during the summer of '69.

Among the many valuable rings displayed in store windows, notice the ones with several diamonds and others with a large single stone setting—usually engagement rings. The girl who gets one treasures her prize. She will value it so much that she will wear it everywhere. But unfortunately a ring can be lost unknowingly. Handwashing causes many a ring to slip off unnoticed because wet fingers are slippery. A ring that gets into the drainage system will be gone forever. But one lost on a playground, picnic area, beach, or in a backyard, stands a good chance of being found again. A coin or a ring dropped on a hard surface will be recovered quickly, but one that falls on gravel or soil will not be found unless somebody searches the area with a metal detector or puts the entire mess through a sieve.

In general, random searching for rings involves too much work. The area of search must be narrowed. With engagement rings you get some help. Owners usually offer sizeable rewards for the return of these sentimental mementos, and they often remember the area of loss.

To get started, turn to the classified ad sections of the local newspaper every day. Read the lost-and-found column. A girl who loses a valuable engagement ring will, because of what it means to her, try to regain that particular ring instead of money from an insurance company. A desperate young lady might run a newspaper ad for several days, offering a reward for return of her ring. Your mission will be to get the reward. But first collect the needed information.

From the owner, get the approximate location of the loss and the kind of activity she was engaged in at the time. In other words, find out if she was playing golf, beach ball, and so on. A good lead at this point and know-how with your detector will make collecting the reward almost a formality.

There is another way to get money from lost rings. It is not romantic or daring but it does get results for some people. This is to take further advantage of reward possibilities. Jewelry is often insured against loss. If so, it becomes an insurance problem the instant it disappears. When the insurance company pays a claim, the lost item becomes its property. This is where the expert with a metal locator comes in. He can offer to work on a percentage basis, and 50 percent of the wholesale value of the jewelry is not unfair.

To start such a service, tell insurance people that you are available to search for lost rings and other similar jewelry. Send out a business card or a letter. The letter should be short. Simply mention the service offered. Write to each company in the phone book in the yellow pages which offers general coverage insurance.

As a beginner and until you get at least a year's experience, operate on the no-find, no-pay basis. Business will be brisker if the other fellow knows he has nothing to lose.

The Hobby That Makes Adventure Profitable

Speaking of losing, just one word of caution. Where money is concerned, misunderstandings often occur between people with the best intentions. This is why people in the business world agree to contracts. It should not be necessary to secure a written contract for each search for lost jewelry you undertake, but it would be an excellent practice to work with a banker.

There are banks everywhere. The people who run them are always helpful, especially to those who have accounts. If you do not have an account, by all means open one and use this action as an opportunity to have a talk with the bank manager or a vice-president. Come right out and tell him you are in the business of recovering lost rings and jewelry and would like to return such items to their owners through the bank. Such experienced bank officials will easily work out an arrangement that will satisfy both you and your clients.

One more word of caution. Inform everybody who inquires about your service of the agent at the bank. Anybody who will not agree to accept delivery through the bank of items which may be recovered is best left alone.

chapter two

Buried Treasures From a Colorful Past

DON'T minimize for one second what brain power can do in the treasure-hunting business. It will, for instance, provide the only dependable help in searching for leads.

It takes work not only to dig for large or small treasures, but also to ferret out the facts and information which tell where the booty is buried or hidden. Happily, a mountain of information about lost mines, hidden Spanish gold, and pirate loot is available, although scattered country-wide in libraries, museums, and national archives. Because of this scattering, most libraries have specialized services to dig up facts for people in need of the information. And for the really tough cases, professional researchers will undertake to build a folio on almost any treasure you can think of. People like Ted Remick of Cleveland, Ohio and Bob Fleming of Arlington, Virginia make a specialty of locating hard-to-find information. Researchers such as Ted and Bob can revive a lagging project.

Research Aids

Those who plan to follow the advice to look first for treasure hoards around home will need to uncover certain special information about their community and surrounding areas. It may be possible to get the information neatly packaged from somebody, but self-reliance produces the best results.

Newspaper Files

Newspaper files help a lot in developing local treasure leads. To get at them, make use of the largest nearby library. Go to the person in charge of the general reference department. Ask to be shown how to use the newspaper file. Most large libraries have their newspaper archives on microfilm. With luck, this type of quick reference method may be available. It can save many hours of work. Choose a time when weather makes outdoor treasure-seeking impossible to dig into library records.

Special Collections

Newspaper morgues do not hold all the answers. Other library sources can be extremely valuable. Historical society collections, for instance, abound with treasure leads for those who learn to recognize the tell-tale stories. History books contain lots of clues, as do biographical works and diaries, published and private.

Watch for special library collections which are financed by trust funds. Such accumulations often contain crucial information.

In doing research, guard against the distractions of interesting recent history. It is easy to be caught up by the past as the decades pass. All kinds of exciting events and interesting information pop up to compete with treasure clues for your attention. Don't, for instance, be sidetracked by stories such as the *Titanic* diasaster during a hunt for the details of a payroll robbery or the site of a forgotten trading post.

Treasure leads in newpaper articles, historical collections, and biographical sketches do not surrender their secrets to a casual reader. But screening these accounts with treasure in view can unearth a hot lead at any time. Of course, staying cool when this happens requires firm self-discipline. Keep a calm exterior even though you feel like shouting, not only when browsing in a library but also when work in the field turns up something research pointed out.

The same stories which lead everybody to buy the daily newspaper—activities of people in public service, wars, natural disasters, and crimes—furnish clues to alert treasure hunters. These news elements exist in every era. And because these events all generate treasure, material for careful appraisal will always be plentiful.

People have many reasons for hiding money, precious metal, or other negotiables. These hoards become potential treasure trove the instant their owners forget what they hid or where they concealed it. Every generation produces men with something to hide. These people usually leave only a few clues to the nature and location of their caches. Money hidden as a result of some type of shady behavior is likely to remain undisturbed forever unless found by accident or a clear-thinking treasure hunter. A few years ago this sort of incident, although not common, was at least not unusual.

In some instances large sums of money would accumulate with no safe place to hide it. Savings accounts were, and still are, unsuitable places to store dollars gained in a questionable manner. Bank accounts provide neither secrecy nor the opportunity to make cash withdrawals after banking hours. A person whose pockets are full of cash as a result of wrongdoing wants to keep his loot safe, but within easy reach. What better way to do this than to hide it in the ground.

The temptation to gather in easy money can be too much for human beings to resist; the newspaper files dating far back contain cops-and-robbers stories of bankers, brokers, messengers, executives, gamblers, and racketeers. The list goes on and on to name people who were caught with their pockets full of somebody else's money or were chased off before they could recover their loot from an underground hiding place. In many instances, the money is still there.

Scan news accounts for items which report loss of funds by other than armed robbery. In an embezzlement case, for instance, the thief often hides stolen money a bit at a time over a period of many years. As the years pass, such a cache might become a sizeable treasure. One frightening day, the culprit learns he is discovered. Then, because of a sudden need to escape imprisonment, he might run away or actually go to prison. In either case, he leaves the scene of the crime. Years and years of accumulated loot remain behind.

Millions of dollars lie in unmarked and unmapped hiding places, the original owners now forgotten or unknown. But careful and patient brainwork, some legwork, and luck will often reveal to a persevering treasure hunter excellent clues to the location of rich and forgotten treasure caches. Discoveries are made by accident, but the treasure hunter who uncovers many finds is obviously doing some thinking.

Maps

Maps do not usually pinpoint the location of treasure, but they can help. A list of maps for treasure hunters would include the topographic series printed by the United States Geological Survey. These detailed maps show individual buildings, and depict ground slope and watershed. Ruins and abandoned buildings are shown along with roads and trails which often do not appear on standard road maps.

The value of a topographic map to a treasure hunter lies in the outdated information which it discloses to a careful viewer. Such maps help in locating old country school sites, for instance. Treasure hunters can pinpoint a school where no building has stood for 20-30 years and locate ghost towns also, especially on maps made from a fifty-year-old survey. The drafting of these maps is such a big job that cartographers have not yet entirely mapped the United States in the topographic series. Until this is done, the updating of older maps probably will not get much attention—fortunately for treasure hunters, who can never get their hands on enough old material.

Excellent map collections can be found in atlases. Map atlases come in various styles and display statistical information as well as simple road and physical features. They begin at township level and go through county and state displays. Again, the old ones are the most helpful. Older atlases reveal the names and exact locations of towns and villages which have disappeared completely—a real boon to treasure hunters. Such places abound in coins, jewelry, and relics. To pick out the towns and villages that have ceased to exist, merely compare an old township or county atlas with a current issue. This method can produce impressive results in areas where logging camps thrived or gold, silver, or copper mines built large communities.

Treasures of the Indians

Don't overlook books, pamphlets, and atlases which detail the location of Indian villages, ceremonial sites, and battlegrounds. Before the white man pushed them into out-of-the-way corners, the American Indians got their hands on great sums of money, some in gold and some in silver. Where did it go? Most of it went right back into the outstretched hands of white traders. The remaining gold and silver specie held by the Indians simply disappeared, probably lost by accident. *It is now in the ground*.

Digging into local Indian history makes an excellent winter project. Locate trails, village sites, and trading posts in your county. Later a metal detector search of ground once used by Indians and traders will produce samples of the gold

Scuba divers discovered these fur trade goods on the Minnesota-Ontario border between Basswood Lake and Crooked Lake, below a rapids on the Basswood River. Shown are 35 Hudson's Bay Company type axeheads, 24 chisels and spears, and a copper trade kettle.—*Photo courtesy Minnesota Historical Society*

1801 Peace Medal.—*Photos courtesy Kenneth White, Sr.*

Shown here are both faces of one of the peace medals given by Lewis and Clark to various Indian chiefs along their route. This one was found by a metal detector in the ground on an Indian battle site in Montana.

and silver coins and medals used to pay the chiefs for cession of territory to the federal government.

Silver Hoard of the Shawnees

In the southwestern part of Ohio a great silver collection once owned by the Shawnee Indian nation lies buried. It represents generations of accumulated tribal wealth.

This treasure was shrewdly hidden by Chief Black Hoof. It resists detection even today. Eventually, this hoard will be found. And it may well be dug up by the person who finds just one more clue in one more old book, or gets a better idea than the other searchers. A cache such as this one could hardly have been retrieved without stirring up a lot of publicity. There is no record of such a commotion, and the chances are that this carefully hidden treasure still lies where crafty old Black Hoof ordered it dumped. The silver went into a nearby marsh—a trick which kept the hiding place secret for more than 100 years. Today the marsh is well drained, and careful detective work will be required to separate possible sites from improbable ones.

The marsh was located near the village of the Shawnees called Chillicothe. Do not confuse this settlement with the large present-day town of Chillicothe. The Indians lived west and north of the existing town located on the east bank of Little Miami River.

The tribe was getting ready to run for its life, for George Rogers Clark was advancing on the Shawnee village with an army of 1000 men. Understandably, the Indians wanted to travel as lightly loaded as possible. Therefore into the swamp went guns and other weapons. All kinds of utensils and tools followed the weapons, and on top of all went hundreds and hundreds of pounds of pure silver. Most of it, too heavy to carry, was in the form of personal ornaments, but a great quantity of plain silver lumps went into the bog along with everything else.

Allan W. Eckert, author of historical novels, reports checking the area over with a mine detector without success. A mine detector, however, has limitations for this type of searching. A deep-search transmitter-receiver metal detector is the instrument of choice in this instance (see Chapter 5).

The approach would be to use a good beat frequency metal detector to locate the path from the village site to the old marsh area which is now drained. If the general area of the cache could be found, the next step would be to go over it carefully with the deep-search transmitter-receiver detector.

Ownership of this Shawnee treasure cache could stir many disputes, for it is no doubt a target worth a great amount of money. Relics from this deposit would be almost priceless, being part of a national treasure.

Treasure-hunting Success Stories

Careful research will no doubt furnish the final clues which will lead to the exact location of the Shawnee treasure. Meanwhile, similar research is providing treasure hunters with action and exciting finds in every category. Here are a couple of examples:

Mr. Donald J., a resident of Linden, Michigan acted on a tip about an abandoned village—that the location was a "short" distance north and that the name of it may have been Deerfield or Elkton.

Starting with this scanty information, Don first visited the library. He dusted off old county records and searched yellowed atlases in the library archives. But the effort ran into a dead end; there was no record of a Deerfield or Elkton in that county. Next, Donald began reviewing microfilm of early area newspapers. The microfilms were full of all kinds of interesting things, but there was no information about the lost village. Finally, just as he was about to shelve the project, he fell over the first solid clue. It appeared on the back page of a forty-year-old newspaper—a small item about an old house burning to the ground the night before. *It was the last house remaining from the village of Elk.* A ten-line history and location of the village ended the news item. The location given identified the town as the elusive community that Don had been searching for.

Armed with his new knowledge, Donald soon learned that the town was in fact known by two names. The second name was new to him, and the designation of Elk was used only to name the post office.

Brush and high weeds hampered preliminary exploration of the site with metal detectors, but Don recovered a few relics such as a logging chain, a crosscut saw, some small pieces of silverware, and some copper jewelry. The recovery of these relics convinced Don that he had located the old townsite and amply justified a systematic search of the area with induction balance and transmitter-receiver types of metal locators (see Chapter 5).

In many instances, ghost towns contain abandoned buildings. These old homes, taverns, and hotels hide a lot of equally old, but highly spendable cash. We can expect to locate and recover much of it, because it is hidden in predictable places. Buried treasure caches, too, reflect patterns of thinking that are predictable.

Mr. M. P. purchased a metal detector to test a treasure story his full-blooded Indian wife had been repeating for many years. She frequently related a story of how she, as a young girl of nine years, had watched her father bury a large sum of money in glass jars. As tribal chief, he was also tribal treasurer. The money he buried was a United States government payment for certain land treaties. The tribe was dispersed at the time and distribution of the money impossible. Therefore, the chief followed the safest course he knew and that was to put the cash in the "bank."

The chief's daughter, now well advanced in years, not only witnessed burial of the money-filled glass jars, but added a modest treasure from her small collection of coins, mostly pennies. Not only did she remember the event, but she was certain of the location. Unfortunately, everybody who heard the story was just as certain that the tale was only a family tradition. One day Mr. P. decided to prove or disprove the story once and for all. The new detector he had just purchased should make the job easy, or so he thought.

The old property was easy to find and it was reasonably free of brush. The building foundations were visible and stones from the well still formed a neat circle. This was important, because the well was one of the points of reference remembered for sixty-plus years. They found nothing. Not even a bottle cap or a copper arrowhead. Mr. P. didn't know whether to say "I told you so" or feel disappointed, but Mrs. P. didn't falter for an instant. She asked her husband whether he was sure he knew how to run the detector. When Mr. P. admitted that he could probably use more practice, Mrs. P. decided to ask the salesman from whom her husband had bought the metal locator to help provide that practice.

Mr. G., the helpful young man who sold the couple their beat frequency metal locator, began by drawing imaginary straight lines from the well site, marked by the stone circle, to each previous building site, marked by crumbling stone foundations. Half a day was then spent with the detector, checking the imaginary paths without result. Mr. P. was beginning to feel a bit smug. But, wisely, he said nothing. It was a good decision. The first coins to be dug from the ground were long out of circulation—Indianhead pennies, seven of them. This was the "little" treasure buried by the chief's 9-year-old daughter. Then the search party discovered a real bonanza—27,000 silver dollars. None of the coins were more than seven inches below the surface, some only a scant three inches under the grass.

Glass shards from the burial containers still lie scattered in the soil of the farmyard. Sixty years of alternate freezing and thawing broke the jars and scattered the coins around many square yards. Some may even have risen to the surface only to be reburied by the first spring rain.

Don't try to dig this story out of the 1969 newspapers. No one but descendants of the Indians covered by the old treaty knows the full story. Although some questions remain to be answered, it might not be polite to ask again; maybe not even safe.

Ghost Towns and Abandoned Fort Sites

Why are empty buildings in ghost towns such good places for hunting treasure? Stopping to think about the reasons why people abandoned towns helps answer this question. Mines ran out of ore; forests were cut down. The towns and villages attached to these industries died as the money stopped flowing across store countertops. The people of these towns, faced with poverty, hoarded every penny. Sometimes they hid their cash reserve close at hand, under steps and in cupboards. Much of it was buried in backyards. To this day remnants of these treasures still await recovery.

Abandoned fort sites, rich in military relics, are common throughout the states of the old Northwest Territory. Ghost towns or abandoned townsites—found occasionally in Michigan, Wisconsin, and Minnesota—are even more numerous in the West. But there is excellent treasure and relic potential in every area.

Treasure on the Pioneer Trails

Think for a moment about the pioneer trails that at one time guided sod busters, settlers, and military forces into the Far West. If you were a lone traveler in a wild and hostile land, how would you keep valuables safe during a night's rest? Chances are you would bury them—coin purse, wallet, or money bag. You would pick a spot within sight, dig a shallow

Buried Treasures from a Colorful Past 33

hole, drop in the wallet or whatever there was to hide, then erase all signs of the burial. The next day you would recover the valuables by remembering the location of the cache in relation to trees, boulders, or other ground features. Settlers, would-be gold miners, and plain adventurers did just that as they fought, rode, or walked their way into the West. Such large numbers of people migrated westward that if only one-tenth of 1 percent of their buried valuables was forgotten or lost, then every foot of the roads they traveled is today a potential treasure site.

Of course, in some places modern roadbeds cover those old military roads and wagon trails. But this is not necessarily a setback. Even in the 1700s or 1800s anybody with sense would camp off the road, usually in a small clearing or by a stream or a lake. The people of a century or two ago loved comfort just as much as their cousins of today. So with comfort in view, pioneers chose overnight rest spots for their nearness to water, safety, and ease of setting up camp. Using these guidelines, today's treasure hunter can, by traveling roads which today follow the early trails, accurately locate old wayside stopover places.

Some of these clearings are now public parks, while others support motels or summer cottages. But in such cases, a courteous talk with a park manager or a property owner will usually result in permission to explore the grounds for evidence of past use by pioneers and settlers. You may even get some unexpected help.

Outlaws' Caches

As the frontier moved west, the white men used wagons at first for transport and then railroads. Loaded wagons and freight trains became rich prizes for thieves, and as commerce moved west, outlaws of several races blazed away at the slow-moving freight haulers and solitary stagecoaches.

Ghost Towns Legend

Arizona

1. White Hills
2. Eagle City
3. La Paz
4. Oro Blanco
5. Kofa
6. McCabe
7. Hilltop
8. Metcalf
9. Jerome
10. Goldroad

California

1. Humbug
2. Deadwood
3. Hayden
4. Englemine
5. Hayfork
6. Washington
7. Knoxville
8. Fiddletown
9. Monro
10. Mt. Bullion
11. New Idria
12. Cerro Gorda
13. Bismarck
14. Dale
15. Walker

Colorado

1. Bachelor
2. Silverton
3. St. Elmo
4. Kokomo
5. Gladstone

Montana

1. Maiden
2. Beartown
3. Wickes
4. Pardee
5. Marysville
6. Rimini
7. Granite
8. Elkhorn

Nevada

1. Contact
2. Jumbo
3. Leadville
4. Relief
5. Joy
6. Ward
7. Goldyke
8. Pine Grove
9. Simon
10. Delmar
11. Gold Mountain
12. Rhyolite
13. Jonnie
14. Arlanta
15. Dolly Varden

Idaho

1. Florence
2. Leesburg
3. Thunder
4. Bullion
5. Springtown
6. Caribou
7. Gem
8. Silver City

New Mexico

1. Mogollon
2. Shakespeare

Oregon

1. Bourne
2. Granite
3. Susanville
4. Auburn
5. Browntown
6. Williams
7. Hardman
8. Cornucopia

Utah

1. Mercur
2. Goldhill
3. Diamond City
4. Newhouse
5. Frisco

Washington

1. Sultan
2. Indes
3. Blewett Pass
4. Trinity

Wyoming

1. Atlantic City
2. Lewistown
3. Alny
4. Bear
5. South Pass

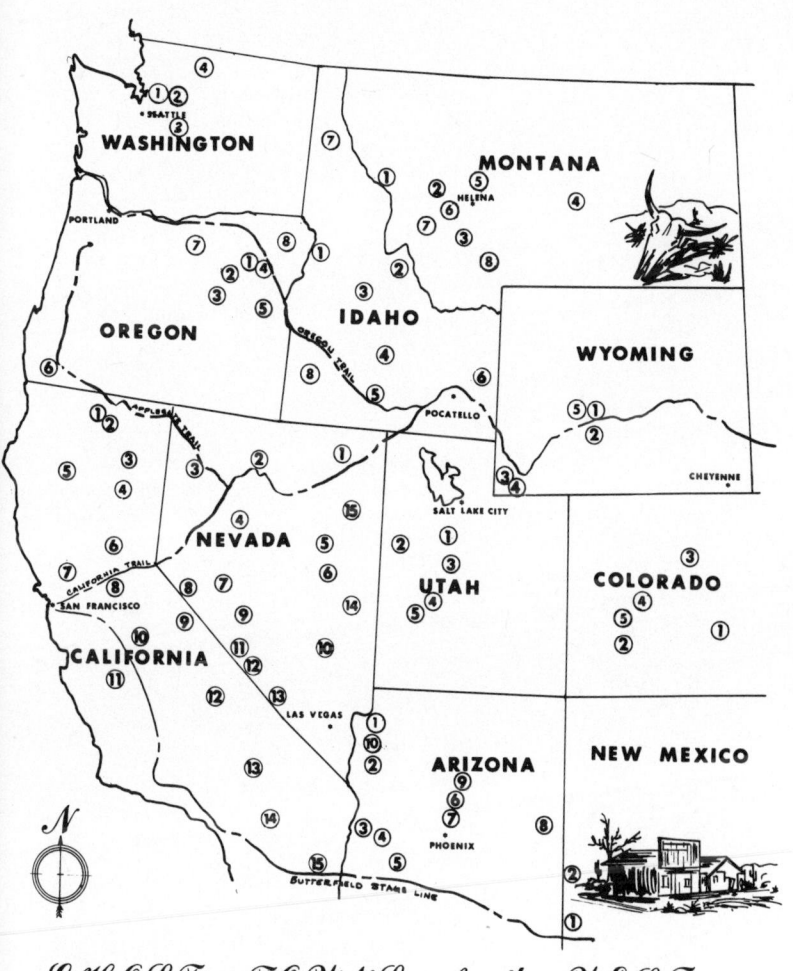

GHOST TOWNS of the WEST

Passengers and drivers were robbed at gunpoint. Often the bandits found their loot too heavy to carry and quickly buried it right on the spot or close by. Today many of the caches which remain underground will become treasure trove to a lucky finder.

Cave-in-Rock

To explore an outstanding example of an authentic robbers' roost, go to southeastern Illinois. This easy-to-find hideout consists of a huge pocket in the face of a limestone cliff on the Illinois-Kentucky border. The old place is called "Cave-in-Rock," and the state of Illinois has dedicated a state park which includes the cave. Now Cave-in-Rock State Park keeps the robbers' lair in custody of the Illinois Conservation Department for generations of visitors yet to come.

Getting to Cave-in-Rock is easy if you live upstream on the Ohio River. Just float downstream to the site of the park. Pull your boat well up on the gray river sand and look up at the cave. To take care of people who cannot use the river,

Cave-in-Rock—*Photo courtesy Illinois State Historical Library*

State Highway No. 1 drops like a loose kite string from Chicago, straight down to the park. Today the cave is a landmark for treasure hunters.

Try to arrive in the spring just after the rainy season. When the water drops to normal level, it often leaves behind or exposes a variety of booty on the beach. Even coins are likely to show up after a heavy rain in summer or fall. Pieces of jewelry, spent bullets, knives, and guns have been found in this area, all dating back to frontier days. (Note: Although at the time of writing treasure hunting is allowed on the beach, things could change.)

During the violent years of the eighteenth- and nineteenth-century frontier in the old Northwest, the cave sheltered pirates from the river and outlaws from all points of the compass. The accumulation of loot from hundreds of robberies and from pirate action on the Ohio River literally became a burden to the outlaws. A horse can carry only so much weight. Consequently, huge amounts of gold, silver, and jewels may be buried in the vicinity of the cave. Considerable treasure has already been recovered from the surrounding area, but there is probably more left than has been retrieved.

Bootleggers' Caches

More recent caches of ill-gotten gains resulted from prohibition. The Volstead Act, passed over President Woodrow Wilson's veto in October of 1919, outlawed intoxicating beverages but made illegal alcohol profitable. By 1921 policemen everywhere were trying to stop the flow of under-the-counter spirits.

Certain types of odd behavior would often tip off government agents to the location of an illegal alcohol still. Also, the smell of fermenting grain would draw the Federal men like bees to a sugar bush. On other occasions unlawful locations would be betrayed by paid informers or rival businessmen.

Federal investigators and local lawmen usually did a great job of destruction on illegal stills as well as the associated apparatus. They smashed everything in sight. But anything below ground usually went undetected. In some instances the below-ground booty is still where it was left on the day of reckoning. The most common item hidden in this manner was payoff money.

During prohibition days and in this particular kind of business, all suppliers demanded cash. But these men who made money with corn liquor and other squeezings were pretty swift fellows who rarely kept more than a few dollars on their person. Most of each day's sales receipts went into hiding. In some cases these hiding places have never been disturbed since the last raid.

If there are any old still sites in your area, careful work can reveal their location. Simply dig into the local library's file of old newspapers starting with a date of 1921. Be on the alert for reports of police raids. They will fall into one of two main types: raids made on alcohol makers and raids made on users. As a treasure hunter, your aim will be to locate long-forgotten places where still operators boiled their mash and bottled the drippings from many coiled copper stills.

Newspaper accounts of police raids on stills usually give accurate details about location. In many cases they pinpoint the exact spot where the apparatus operated. Once the place is found, use a metal locator to find the below-ground caches. Make a locator search around the base of all large trees and posts of any kind. Look for clues to hiding places such as posts set in a square, circle or other pattern. Remember also that even copper pipes bring $.30 a pound.

Money Caches of Bernarr MacFadden

The habit of hiding money underground was (and is) not limited to the world of outlaws. Legitimate businessmen sometimes use holes in the ground to hide large sums of money. One such individual was well known during his lifetime as a publisher. His name: Bernarr MacFadden.

At one time the name Bernarr MacFadden was close to being a household word. This man accumulated a large personal following by advocating physical exercise to keep the body healthy. He also accumulated a lot of money. So much, in fact, that he only felt comfortable with it buried underground, out of sight.

Bernarr apparently had little use for banks. He carried a suitcase as he traveled around, full of large-denomination bills. Now and then he would stop to bury some of this money. Bernarr used heavy army surplus ammunition cans to hold the cash. He would seal the packaged cans with a waterproof cover and bury them where he could get at them in a hurry if he should need money. One, perhaps two, of these caches has been located. Some patient research on the travels of this once famous person might turn up important clues to a great fortune.

Posthole Banks

Similar buried treasure caches literally abound all over the United States. There is, for instance, an intriguing treasure cache possibility in every farmyard fifty years old or more. These potential hot spots are called posthole banks. And many such old banks have not had a withdrawal in forty years.

Farmers and even some city dwellers used posthole banks to keep cash reserves from thieves and even from members of their own family. One man might have reason to bury money because a tender-hearted wife would lend cash to an unemployed relative. Another might want to avoid paying the bill collectors. Another might just like money. Anyway, if there was no cash in the house, it would be quite difficult to give it away or pay it out. The big question was where to hide money so it would be safe from intruders or accidental discovery, and yet be there for the owner to get at quickly.

A posthole bank filled the need very well. Such a bank is simply the space below one specially prepared post in part of a fence row. To remember the post easily, the depositor would locate it first or second from a corner close to a building or tree. Or he might nail a horseshoe or some other item of scrap hardware on the side or top, or cut a notch in the wood to signify the importance of that particular pole.

To provide for quick recovery in case of need, the depositor sometimes kept the post separate from the fence wire. In any event, he made the post to fit the hole snugly but yet be easy to lift out. A post where all the wires have been spliced or where there is an unusual amount of slack in the wires often indicates the presence of a posthole bank. Below the post, the depositor placed a container to hold the cash or other treasure. There it would be kept secure in a glass jar or sealed in a hot-water bottle.

Alert treasure hunters quite regularly make withdrawals from forgotten posthole bank deposits.

Old Farm Dumps

While looking around abandoned farmyards for posthole banks, don't forget the deserted old farm dumps. After locating the metal mass of a dump with a detector, it is easy to excavate the old bottles and other relics once thought to be worthless junk. Just about anything that illustrates our forebears' way of life is called Americana. To learn what is and what is not valuable, visit a flea market which permits browsing at leisure. The proprietors of these highly mobile outlets for scarce and ancient relics are well informed about the worth of such merchandise. If you state your purpose honestly, they will provide tips on the kind of relics to concentrate on in your particular area. An item such as an ancient inkwell or a worn horseshoe might find a buyer, but old silverware and cast-off toys are sure to garner tidy sums.

Treasures That Armies Left Behind

Treasure hunters who are looking for military relics rather than money will do well to examine the sites of battles and other military operations, such as forgotten campgrounds. It might pay to search along the route of Morgan's Raid, a military expedition of particular interest to treasure hunters which took place during the Civil War.

Confederate General John Hunt Morgan rose from a relatively junior post as a captain at the war's beginning to major-general by 1863. His specialty: guerrilla warfare. It was to bring him much fame and considerable trouble. The fame came to Morgan from incredible success as a raider and an ability to outguess generals of the Northern forces that chased him at top speed. Morgan's trouble came from simply pushing his luck too far. But the end did not come until after he carried out the most daring and successful guerrilla attack of the Civil War.

It started at Burkesville, Kentucky on July 2, 1863 and ended at Beaver Creek, Ohio twenty-four days later. In those twenty-four days Morgan traveled over 500 miles and gave the North a fright that is still remembered.

Buried Booty from Morgan's Raid

Ahead of the raiders (who probably conducted the most gentlemanly raid in the history of warfare), worried citizens buried everything from the family silver to uncle Ned's new shoes. The raiders themselves were losing things at a record rate. After all, there is only limited space on a horse's back and some of the accumulated battle spoils simply fell off to be lost in fields, rivers, and in ditches along the road. During the tense nights pilfering soldiers undoubtedly buried many

valuable items to prevent the true owners from ever recovering them. Except what has been found by accident in the years since the Civil War, it is all still there.

Many skirmishes were fought along the route. Tebbs Bend, Kentucky witnessed the first of many battles to come for Morgan. He could not have picked a fight in a more unfavorable spot. The Twenty-fifth Michigan Infantry was secured in a solid little fort. The Green River and high banks protected the sides and Morgan was left with only two choices: a head-on attack or going around. He chose to fight and gained nothing but grief.

This small battlefield might yield excellent military relics to a search with electronic detecting equipment. A mile upstream from Tebbs Bend, a search at the place where Morgan crossed the river with 2000 men on horseback might prove rewarding.

Damage caused by General Morgan and his troops on this

wide sweep into Northern territory exceeded the sum of $25 million. His own losses were also very great. Perhaps one of the most spectacular operations in terms of material loss occurred on the Ohio-Kentucky border. In hope of crossing the Ohio River at the ford below Buffington Island, General Morgan drove himself and his men to use their last reserves of strength in an attempt to make this final crossing. But Morgan's Raid really came to an end at Buffington Island. Although Morgan and a few others escaped the battle at this place, he lost most of his equipment and supplies in addition to all the loot picked up in the long ride into Indiana and Ohio.

One newspaper man who walked around the Buffington Island area after the battle reported the "battlefield was strewn with merchandise and knickknacks." At another place, "wagons and carriages were strewn about in a vast tangle. Arms and ammunition littered the area, adding to the sadness of the survivors."

Today, historical plaques mark the battlefield at Buffington Island and Portland. Souvenir hunting in the park area is discouraged, but private land nearby has relic potential. Land owners in historic areas will usually allow nondestructive exploration on their property. The entire area from Pomeroy to Long Bottom should repay such investigation.

Other Civil War Treasures

Buried treasure of Civil War origin can be found anywhere that the war touched the civilian population. It also lies where people very much involved with the war hid it. Rumor has it that someone from this last group hid a $2,000,000 army payroll near Kingsland, Georgia. And near Demopolis, Alabama, an unknown sum of money was buried on the Whitefield farm. Despite the recovery of a portion of this Civil War treasure in 1925, more probably remains.

The state of Tennessee is host to one of the more commonly known, though lost, Civil War treasures—war loot hidden by soldiers and reported to be worth over a million dollars. This often looked-for treasure is thought to be buried near Owl Creek just a mile and a half northeast of the Henderson County town of Lexington. A metal locator should help on this one.

The Treasure of Hermit Island

Military operations of other eras have also left behind items of interest to today's treasure seekers. Somewhere on Hermit Island in the Apostle group in Lake Superior British soldiers reputedly buried an army payroll for overnight safekeeping. At this time during the early 1700s in the area of western Lake Superior, the natives were restless all the time. Hostile Indians overwhelmed the small party of soldiers who were transporting the payroll. Except for a few lucky escapes, no one survived. It is not likely that the Indians took the payroll, however. They were after the red coats of the British soldiers. Later search parties were unable to locate the buried payroll before the ever prowling Indians chased the treasure seekers away. Today, a good metal detector should be able to locate this treasure.

If you plan to seek out Hermit Island for a look at the treasure possibilities, get the owners' permission. Thousands of acres are open to public use in the Apostles, but privately owned Hermit Island is not included.

Although the federal and state lands in the Apostles are classed for recreational use, get the latest regulations concerning land use before unpacking your treasure hunting gear to explore for the other treasures reported hidden on the islands. Address inquiries to Department of Natural Resources, P.O. Box 589, Bayfield, Wisconsin 54814.

Hidden gold everywhere beckons treasure hunters, especially those with hot leads to specific targets, but, remember, it is easy to miss the goal if you get too involved in the chase.

chapter three

The Hidden Riches of American Beaches

WHAT can match the romance and excitement of buried pirate gold? The pirates famed in legend were as wild a bunch of rascals as the world has ever seen. Yet strangely enough, their fierceness helped to save the rather weak North American governments from the burden of permanent Spanish rule.

Many pirates of the late seventeenth century, known as buccaneers, differed from the pirate bands which appeared in later years. These buccaneers had once lived in peace, but were driven to piracy by the cruelty of the Spaniards.

Previously to their life as pirates, the buccaneers enjoyed a thriving business of smoke-curing dried meat. Curiously enough, this activity gave buccaneers their name. They cured beef by smoking long strips over a smudge fire. When cured by this method, beef would keep indefinitely. The Carib Indians who originated the process, used the word *"boucan"* to indicate the place for smoke-drying meat. The term *"boucaneers"* referred to the men doing the work. It stayed with them after they stopped their smoking trade and went on to the piracy business. In later years the name was worked over by English-speaking sailors and it became what it is today: buccaneers.

Exploits of the Buccaneers

The buccaneers brought cold fear to all captains of the Spanish Main, not to mention a few under the French flag. Primarily, the buccaneers organized to protect the American coast from the aggressive Spaniards, who were at the time planning to take over all the Americas. Their fierce attacks met with great success and eventually forced Spain to depend upon convoys to get gold-laden ships back to home ports.

A bit of action which illustrates the aggressive nature of these restless men began April 5, 1680. On this day, 330 buccaneers under the leadership of Bartholomew Sharp joined with him to begin a long campaign against the Spaniards. This private war took Sharp and his men on a hike across the Isthmus of Panama and then to the Pacific Ocean. There, after stealing a boat, they sailed south along the coast of South America. Eventually they groped their way past the Strait of Magellan, around the Tierra del Fuego, and into the South Atlantic, raiding the coast along the way. From that southernmost point of the Americas, the buccaneers turned and sailed north until they arrived once again in the Caribbean and home base. It was then January 28, 1682.

During nearly two years of continuous action, one thing drove them on—gold. They never turned down silver and jewels, of course, but they generally buried all of the silver bullion and special cargo or threw it into the sea. Space aboard ship was limited, and therefore gold held all the priorities.

Sometimes buccaneers earned their gold from legitimate employment. They were often employed as crews on privately owned warships in the service of governments then trying to trade with the Americas. It was a quick route to a cheap navy. The problem which resulted for everyone, of course, was that of keeping track of who was fighting whom. The cheap navy was an attractive idea, but it failed completely. The pirates, living up to their reputation, could not resist attacking any ship that would yield a profit. In the process of robbing honest merchantmen—and often one another—of gold, silver, and jewels, these outlaws gathered in a huge pile of treasure. Their greed signaled the beginning of the end. Ironically, the buccaneers were eventually put completely out of business by the navies of England and France, the same nations that earlier gave these fellows their starting push.

Buried Pirate Gold

While these buccaneers were fierce and terrible at sea, they met their match when it came to dealing with shopkeepers, tavern owners, and other peddlers. It didn't take long for the news to travel along the Atlantic Coast that a buccaneer and his money were soon parted.

A few cool-headed leaders soon realized that they would be wise to take less money where it could brighten the eyes of shopkeepers. It would be better, they reasoned, to take the loot ashore to hide it; and so hide it they did. Usually, they did the job so well that accidental discovery of the treasure would be impossible. Often a pirate leader could be seen returning alone from a trip inland to bury booty—the work crew being left at the cache site to guard it forever.

Pirates of the eighteenth century buried plenty of gold in the plate and bar form called bullion as well as in coined money called specie. They also left a trail of sorts to the location of their treasure caches. To find these clues, simply pick a likely pirate leader and begin a folio of information gathered from records of his life and travels.

Blackbeard, as he appeared in engraving in Captain Charles Johnson's *General History of the Lives and Adventures of the Most Famous Highwaymen Murderers and Pyrates*, published in London in 1734.—*Photo courtesy the Harry Elkins Widener Collection, Harvard University Library*

Most people know the names of the most feared of the outlaw sea captains even today. There is Captain Edward Teach, for one. Captain Teach (better known as Blackbeard) had a reputation for excessive cruelty and also for hidden treasures which now lie buried along the Atlantic Coast of the United States. The vain and proud Bartholomew Roberts enjoyed an eventful career. He was killed while at sea and buried there. Thomas Tew loved traveling to far-off places and was also lost at sea during a fight. Captain William Fly lost his life to the hangman's noose, and Captain William Lewis fell out with his crew. Captain Lewis lost the argument and paid with his life. But the pirate whose exploits still make tongues wag after 200 years was Captain William Kidd. Probably no other pirate buried gold, jewels, and pieces of eight in such quantity. Captain Kidd, too, came to a violent end. He was hanged May 23, 1701 in England.

The treasures left by Captain Kidd, as well as by other pirates who sailed the waters of the Americas, lie scattered along both east and west seacoasts. These hoards still rest under the sand and earth of the beaches where they were buried, on islands, and in isolated caves which are difficult if not impossible for a lone person to enter.

Beginners interested in pirate treasure can profit by collecting samples of the great pirate hoards. They wash upon certain beaches of the eastern seaboard and to a lesser extent along the Gulf Coast beaches. In every case, the best hunting occurs after a storm.

Jersey Coast Treasure of Captain Kidd

Captain Kidd reportedly buried his largest treasure hoard on Money Island off the New Jersey coast. In fact, the island, now covered by the sea, got its name and reputation from legends about the treasure of the famous pirate. Today the beaches in this region continue to make good hunting.

A report issued by the New Jersey Coast Committee places

Very early rough *Spanish* earring.—*Photo courtesy Gene Ballinger*

A metal detector found this earring, made of pound silver and adorned with a rough, uncut emerald, on the Mississippi coast.

this treasure area in the water off the beach, east of Toms River and west of Island Heights. Look for a high eminence on the north shore of Toms River. This is a clue to the location of the sunken island.

Where to Find Coins from Shipwrecks

The sea often washes coins and other treasure ashore on both the east and west coasts from the offshore wrecks of pirate vessels and other ships. One of the most dependable places to look for these riches from the sea is a beach a couple of miles south of Wellfleet, Massachusetts. The coins which reach the shore at this spot on Cape Cod probably come from a ship called the *Whidah*, lost here by pirate captain Samuel Bellamy. The *Whidah* carried over $100,000 in gold and silver from Spanish coin mints. Salvage of the wreck was attempted shortly after it went aground and continues even today. But the sea lets go only when it wants to. The treasure is still in the wreck except for what comes ashore on storm waves a few coins at a time.

Delaware's Money Beach

Another money beach is in Delaware. Here the strip of sand where coins turn up extends 9½ miles south from Rehoboth Beach, at the entrance to Delaware Bay. Highway 18 comes in from the west, and a boat is needed to approach from the east. Coins washing ashore on Delaware's money beach probably come from a ship called the *Faithful Steward*. This vessel foundered in 1785 while trying to enter the bay.

Various relics such as personal effects also appear at the water's edge; they probably originate from the same wreck, although there are a couple of other possibilities. The vessel called the *Three Brothers* sank in the same area at about the same time. It may have broken up and its cargo may be washing ashore with whatever is coming in from the *Faithful Steward*.

There is also some possibility that relics and coins appear on this beach from another vessel called the *de Braak*. The wreck of this British war sloop reportedly lies in approximately fifteen fathoms. The *de Braak* turned over and sank off Cape Henlopen, May 1798, with a treasure cargo—possibly worth $10 million—consisting entirely of gold and silver taken at gunpoint from Spanish treasure ships.

As with the *Whidah*, private groups have tried and continue to try to salvage the treasure of the *de Braak*. But there is no record of any great success. The ship lies in the muddy seabed, a very tempting target for treasure hunters. During violent storms cargo may be washed from the wreck, and eventually cast in pieces onto the beaches along this area.

The Bonds Treasure Site

Another possible money beach site occurs on the New Jersey coast. Called the Bonds treasure site, it got its name from the community of Bonds, located in Ocean County on the island of Long Beach, two miles north of the shipwreck involved. The name of the sloop wrecked here is unknown, but it went aground at this spot in 1897 and remained without further incident until several years later. Then at a place on the beach close to the wreck site, two men working within sight of the Little Egg Harbor lifesaving station recovered what was apparently a chest of treasure. The lifesavers chased the treasure hunters off the beach, but the only items left for the pursuers to think about were a chart, a rusty cutlass, and a few old Spanish coins.

Today the beach area near the old lighthouse site should be searched carefully after every storm. You may be surprised at what the sea will give up if you look in the right places.

Washington's Money Beaches

The east coast does not have a monopoly on money beaches. They actually exist quite uniformly wherever the seas and lakes meet land. To find hot spots, look for the lighthouses. They stand on places where ships went ashore before the beacons were erected.

On the west coast, Washington's rugged beaches hide plenty of loot. The area around the mouth of the Quinault River is an excellent hunting ground. Ships have foundered on these rocks since at least the sixteenth century. Even

The Hidden Riches of American Beaches

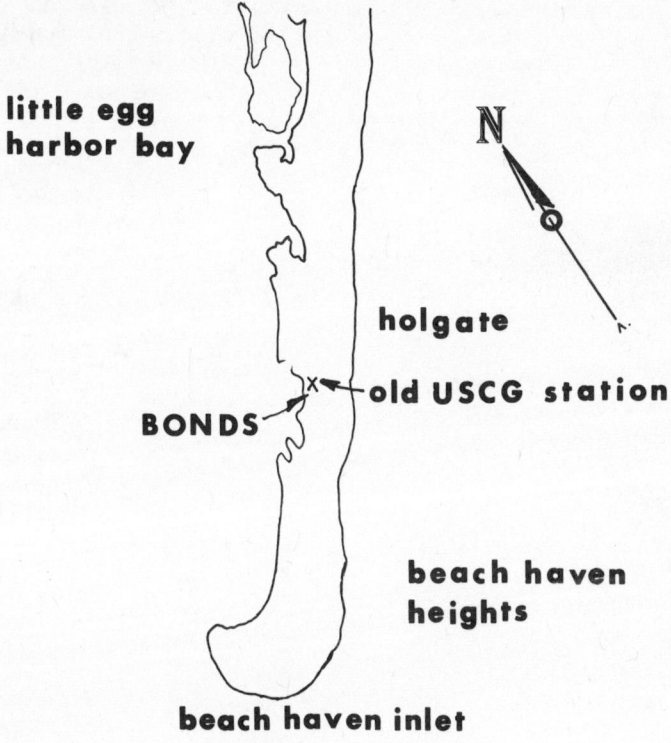

The Bonds treasure site.

Chinese junks have been wrecked on these shores after drifting across thousands of Pacific Ocean miles. Spanish, English, and American ships—possibly several hundred of them—have ended their days on these shores since the mid-1800s. Nobody knows what is hidden there, either in shallow water or just beneath the sand at the tide line.

The Treasures of Padre Island

Perhaps no single strip of sand anywhere in the world conceals more gold, silver, and relics than the beaches of Padre Island, off the coast of Texas. This narrow, curving sliver of dunes, beach sand, and saw grass curves gracefully for more than seventy miles, as though sliced from the mainland with a knife, along the exposed southeastern flank of the state. Against the eastern shore of this island a never still sea constantly works to renew the treasure supply of the sands. The valuables come in from the sea, piece by piece. Most likely, they originate from the ancient wrecks which lie offshore.

In 1553 a fleet of twenty Spanish sailing ships left Mexico for the long trip to Spain, and sailed straight into a hurricane. This twenty-vessel flotilla, the Silver Fleet, got its name from a large shipment of precious metal stored below decks. Only three vessels from this flotilla survived the wild storm which swept across the Gulf of Mexico. The three surviving ships lasted just long enough to be wrecked in the shallows which guard Padre Island. Eventually the wrecked boats disappeared entirely into the sand and sea.

Despite the riches washed ashore on Padre Island, however, the island is not fair game for treasure hunters. It is a National Seashore and subject to the provisions of the Antiquities Act of 1906, with which all treasure hunters should be familiar. Briefly, in the case of Padre Island, it is forbidden to appropriate or excavate any object of antiquity on the island without permission from the Secretary of the Interior. This prohibition applies to fragments of old ships, Spanish pieces of eight, Indian artifacts, Civil War items, and other materials of scientific or historic value which are constantly being removed from the island by treasure hunters taking advantage of lax enforcement of the law.

Nevertheless, treasure hunters do have some legitimate scope for operations on the island. By using their metal detecting equipment, they can pinpoint the locations of historic artifacts and report them to the Padre Island National Seashore office so that properly trained scientists can supervise recovery operations. Treasure hunters should be careful not to remove the items themselves, however, or they will be in violation of the Act.

Treasure of John Singer

One national treasure which modern argonauts might well help find is the collection of John Singer. At the time of the Civil War, John Singer of the Singer Sewing Machine family was living on the island. Singer was a part-time treasure hunter, and, as such, he could hardly have lived in a better spot to practice his hobby. By the time Federal soldiers occupied the island, John had collected almost $100,000 from its sands and dunes.

When the Federal troops came, John Singer escaped in the nick of time, but not before carefully hiding his collection of gold and jewels, supposedly about six miles north of his house on Padre Island. After the war was over and the army gone, John moved back again to the island. Sad to say, he could not relocate his buried treasure cache. It's probably still there.

Treasure hunters will be glad to know that the law permits them to keep those items washed ashore on the island which are not of historic or scientific value. Beachcombers with varied interests have found the hunting good at a place on the island known as the Devil's Elbow, a sort of catch basin where currents combine to collect sea drift of every description—fishing floats to Florida oranges.

The Kennedy Causeway from Corpus Christi provides access to Padre Island. The first ten miles on the island south of Nueces County Park accommodate regular vehicles, but past the ten-mile mark, four-wheel drive vehicles are a must.

The Mystery of Oak Island

Islands seem to have a special charm for people who want to hide money. Just off the coast of Nova Scotia lies Oak Island. It is either the site of an elaborately hidden treasure hoard or the scene of the most cleverly rigged and long-lasting treasure hoax of the last ten centuries. The competent engineer who hid whatever lies at the bottom of the 100-foot-deep shaft on Oak Island went to a lot of trouble for the whole thing to be a fraud.

A fellow named Daniel McGinnis started the treasure hunt in 1795. By accident he discovered a tree on the island that appeared to have been used to support a pulley and rope. McGinnis knew that such devices were used by sailors to lift heavy cargo, and he was quick to imagine what kind of "freight" lay beneath the ground on Oak Island. His imagination infected others.

Help quickly arrived to dig up the vast treasure that McGinnis's mind had pictured. The shovels flashed and the dirt flew. Every ten feet down, the diggers found they had to stop to hack away at a platform made of oak boards. Finally they reached what seemed to be the last platform at the 100-foot level. This happened late in the day and the final step, it was agreed, should be carried out the following morning. In the morning the hole was full of salt water.

And so began one of the most lengthy and expensive treasure hunts of all time. Indefatigable treasure hunters have wasted over a million dollars in a never ending search for the elusive riches of Oak Island. Today on the island, extensive digging has pitted the land with so many deep and shallow holes, nobody knows for certain which is the original shaft.

A new group, Triton Alliance, Ltd., has secured rights to search for the treasure from the island's owner. Perhaps they will have better luck than a gentleman from Los Angeles who is said to have recently spent more than $100,000 in a fruitless attempt to get at the treasure.

Not all hunts for big treasure cause so much frustration as the struggle with Oak Island's money pit. It is always easier, however, to get information about the failures than about the successes.

Treasure hunters can score successes in every state, but some states have more to offer than others. Georgia, for instance, is heavily endowed with buried treasure. Any treasure hunter seriously interested in making recoveries should also investigate Florida, California, Texas, Arizona, Idaho, and Ohio.

Of course, there are many amateur treasure hunters who for many reasons are not able to devote the personal time needed to hunt for the big ones. For these people there is the little treasure approach. Finding a few small but valuable items can add up to one big bonanza.

Happy hunting!

chapter four

Relics and Gold From Lakes and Sea

HALF the refined gold of the entire world lies scattered on sea, lake, and river bottoms. No wonder so many people caught up in the humdrum business of daily life dream of diving into the sea for a chest of gold, silver, and jewels. Treasures exist on wrecked pirate ships, ships of state bearing payroll gold, and modern wrecks with bullion aboard. All seas and rivers of the world, plus the Great Lakes, conceal valuable items of jettisoned cargo.

Sunken treasure is covered by all possible combinations of water and sediment. It's under green water, muddy and clear. It lies in water of wading depth, and in water so deep that ten Empire State Buildings piled one on top of the other from the ocean floor would still not provide a dry place to sit.

Dramatic Salvaging Operations

In recent years, persistent salvagers have recovered great riches from sunken vessels. The importance of persistence in treasure hunting is illustrated vividly by the success of three amateur divers-turned-treasure-hunters who located and cleaned out the eighteenth-century wreck of the French treasure ship *Le Chameau*. The wreck had lain untouched since the day it sank, August 26, 1725, just off the rocky coast of Cape Breton Island, Nova Scotia.

Alex Storm, an employee of the Canadian Northern Affairs Department, researched and searched for the treasure wreck in his spare time for three years. For the last year he was joined by two assistants: Dave MacEachern, also a government employee, and Harvey McLeod, a railroad fireman.

This trio of treasure-hunting amateurs recovered the long-sought $700,000 gold and silver payroll from the hulk of the sunken *Chameau* in the fall of 1966. After the long preliminaries, the actual recovery was ridiculously easy.

Working in total secrecy, these young men stuffed heavy cotton bags full of coins and hauled them seventy feet to the surface. At the end of twenty days, the entire haul was resting safely in the vault of a local bank. Luck? Of course, there is always an element of luck in every successful treasure hunt, but mostly the job was done by people who refused to quit working until the treasure was in their hands.

Almost directly east of Nova Scotia and 2000 miles across the North Atlantic, the ancient wreck of the *Girona* has been forced to yield its treasure. This ship, part of the great armada which Spain assembled for the invasion of England in 1588, sank within sight of land.

Over a period of five months in 1968, salvagers battled the sea and other divers in a contest for the *Girona*'s treasures. They won because they refused to give up. Many of the artifacts recovered from this wreck site are too rare to be priced by ordinary standards.

Thousands of miles to the west of Ireland and England and off the coast of California lies the 1853 wreck of the mail steamer *Winfield Scott*. Skin divers located this one in 1969 and removed a fortune in gold coin. Although the ship was supposed to be carrying an $800,000 shipment of gold coins at the time it sank, salvagers reportedly recovered the money at a later time. Apparently the 1969 divers knew about the cargo but not about the salvage report. They have since been recovering gold coin, without realizing that many years ago somebody else was there before them. This is another example of treasure being where you find it.

Such treasure finds are mere samples of what is going on continually, and there are a lot more yet to be found.

The Lost Golden Galleons of Spain

No sunken treasure has been so eagerly sought as Spanish gold. Estimated in terms of today's values, the Spanish take on the North and South American continents amounted to more than $10 billion in gold, silver, and jewels. To the Spaniards' chagrin, much of this wealth ended up on the bottom of the sea. In fact, a quarter of all the gold and silver mined by the conquistadores in the New World was lost at sea. A tenth of the entire Spanish loot found its way to the bottom of the Atlantic and connecting waters. Of that fraction perhaps one-quarter has been recovered. (Treasure hunters have been at it, remember, for centuries.)

During the mid-sixteenth century, Spain squeezed about $100 million in precious metal and jewels from the treasuries of Central and South America and loaded it aboard great towering galleons for shipment home; two huge armadas sailed each year until the eighteenth century, when the New World colonies began to get restless. Carefully kept Spanish records reveal that 5 percent of the ships which sailed for home with a load of treasure were lost at sea.

Spanish Wrecks in Florida Waters

Pirates and storms at sea both hindered the Spaniards' attempt to transport all their new-found riches to the

Relics and Gold from Lakes and Sea

Some of the treasure salvaged from a Spanish fleet wrecked off present-day Cape Kennedy. Items include two-*escudo* gold piece (held in woman's fingers), and silver pieces-of-eight surrounding a gold cross, a diamond ring, and a magnificent gold necklace with a dragon-fish charm.—*Photo © courtesy National Geographic Society*

homeland. Ironically, the weather took the most plunder from the Spaniards. The Spanish government lost squadron after squadron of ships to hurricanes alone, much of this loss occurring in Florida waters during the years 1501-1820. During a hurricane which hit the Atlantic side of Florida in 1715, ten ships foundered off what is now Cape Kennedy. One ship was blown almost completely out of the water by the wind. Salvagers recovered much of the gold from this vessel after the storm, but it is believed that a large amount remains in the hulk. The *Concepcion* sank in the same area with a cargo worth at least $3 million, and many other wrecks caused by this one storm are clustered in the area of Cape Kennedy. These wrecks have been the object of "fishing" expeditions since the word first leaked out. The salvagers of the Real Eight Corporation, which started operations in the mid-1960s, have recovered much of the treasure from this fleet (about $3 million), but the search continues.

Many of the treasure wrecks off the coast of Florida are in water from eight to twenty feet deep. At these depths, scuba (self-contained underwater breathing apparatus) or face mask and snorkle, together with underwater metal locators, obtains good results. After several hundred years, however, in tropic seas, there is practically nothing left to identify these wrecks as once being ships. Only heaps of stone ballast and a few scattered cannon remain today. But that is sufficient. To the

Old Spanish cannon recovered from the floor of the Caribbean Sea off Florida.—
Photo courtesy Calvin Deviney

Relics and Gold from Lakes and Sea

knowing eye, a ballast heap means a ship and maybe a treasure ship, though only a slow and careful search of the wreck site will tell the story.

Inside three leagues (ten statute miles from shore), Florida requires a license for all treasure-hunting activity, although, at the time of writing, the state's claim to such a limit for its territorial waters has not yet been tested in court. Beyond the three-league limit no restrictions apply. Of course, it is doubtful that every skin diver who sees a coin or two in the shallows rushes off to the capital for a license to pick it up.

Florida issues permits for work on specific wrecks, but these permits are very difficult to obtain and the exact location of a wreck must be given before an application will be considered. The state has been very lax about protecting these locations, however, and this has resulted in pirating by some individuals.

Valuable Sunken Mercury

Valuable cargo was lost going in both directions between Spain and the New World. Approximately a third of all the Spanish ships lost around the Caribbean came from Europe. They were heavily loaded but contained mostly perishable cargoes. Merchandise such as mining equipment, paper, silk, and food was soon destroyed if sunk in the sea. One finished product, however, was very necessary to the New World—and would have survived to this day—namely, the mercury used in refining gold and silver.

As much as 500 tons a year of the mercury shipped from Spain in wooden casks was used to refine gold and silver from crushed ores. A number of mercury shipments went down either in the Caribbean or in the approaches to it. Today this liquid metal would be worth many millions of dollars.

Two ships loaded with mercury went aground on the point of the Samana Peninsula on Hispaniola in August 1724 during a fierce Caribbean hurricane. The two ships, *Guadalupe* and *Tolosa,* should lie in about twenty feet of water. Salvagers recovered part of the mercury cargo from the battered vessels after the wreck. Today, there would be nothing of these ships to mark their resting places except ballast mounds and perhaps a cannon or two close at hand. Although the wooden casks have probably not survived, tons of mercury could still be intact under the sand and stone ballast heaps in pools on bedrock. Its value on today's market is such that recovery of a few barrels would repay the effort many times over.

Deep-Water Treasures

Of course, not all sunken treasure lies in shallow water. Soon, engineers and divers will join hands and minds to go after the deep wrecks. Beyond the three-mile limit, many wrecks lie in deep water just waiting for treasure hunters who refuse to take no for an answer.

In the future, the open sea outside state and federal waters will offer the best opportunities to recover sunken treasure. There, except for income taxes, reporting success or failure is a matter of personal concern. At present, however, although deep-sea wrecks do not pose a problem to anyone who can swim for hours at the 200- to 300-foot level, the rest of us must wait for a scientific breakthrough in self-contained underwater breathing apparatus and better metal detector instruments to pinpoint deep wrecks.

Treasures of the Great Lakes

The ocean has no monopoly on underwater treasures. Fabulous riches lie beneath the waters of the Great Lakes as well—not only gold and silver but artifacts and relics worth huge sums of money. Even wooden planks and beams have special value, if they have been soaking in these waters below the 30-foot-deep ice line for a long time.

Low oxygen, cold, and purity distinguish the fresh waters of Lake Superior. Lake Huron comes close to having the same high-quality water, with Lakes Michigan, Erie, and Ontario next in order. This low oxygen, low temperature, and purity work to preserve rather than corrode all wooden and metal objects immersed in it. Certain wood grains, such as found in the oaks, are actually improved by long soaking in mineralized fresh water. Souvenir desk sets, bookends, and even large pieces of furniture made from salvaged wreck timbers, find a ready and waiting market. Profits available from the sale of souvenirs and other collectibles may not have the clink of gold coins, but it's real money and spends just as quickly.

Wreck of the Westmoreland

Anybody who prefers searching for ordinary gold coins rather than extraordinary oak planks could start with the wreck of the steamer *Westmoreland*. This old steamer sank to the bottom of upper Lake Michigan within easy swimming distance of land—a rare stroke of luck for treasure hunters! Some of the best picnic spots and swim beaches in the Midwest are in this search area. Treasure hunters who get weary of diving for gold or searching for the 100-year-old wreck of the *Westmoreland* can rest in these recreation spots.

In December 1854, mariners feared to sail the Lakes late in the season no less than they do today. Every storm on the Great Lakes during November and December brings the added dangers of ice—not just a slippery coating, but inches-thick tons that can capsize a ship in seconds during a storm.

Present-day insurance companies are apt to refuse to gamble on a ship that sails the Lakes during December. The *Westmoreland,* however, sailed in the days before ship owners gave much attention to considerations of safety. This lack of concern led to a fatal decision to send the ship out on its last trip. Salvagers have made a few attempts to locate the wreck in the vicinity of the Sleeping Bear Sand Dune, a pile of sand that could hardly be improved upon as a landmark.

Today the $100,000 in gold coins reported to be in the ship's safe would be worth several times their face value. In the mid-1800s, gold was the universal language of commerce. Merchants everywhere accepted gold coins, and Great Lakes traders were, as they are today, right in the middle of furious trading activity.

The workhorses of the Lakes were the 160-200-foot lumber hookers, all built from a few common basic designs especially for use on the Lakes. They sailed by the thousands and hauled enough lumber to build hundreds of midwestern towns. These ships also sailed with tons of grain and coal and mountainous deckloads of machinery. Even Christmas trees went over the lakes by the shipload. All this without a single drive-in bank, mail boat, or computer-protected checking account.

Under these conditions cash money talked. Ships' captains carried payment money wherever they went, usually in gold. If the ship sank, the gold sank too, and plenty of these boats did just that. They went to the bottom in hundreds of storms and they took with them uncounted thousands of dollars in specie. The idea today is to locate these wrecks, and initiate salvage of safes and strongboxes. These were usually carried in the captain's cabin.

The wrecks of these boats strew the bottoms of the Lakes from the lower portion of Lake Huron to the farthest point of Lake Michigan. They lie in shallow water on down to the abyssal depths which protect everything from inquisitive human hands.

Here also, while gold has the greatest allure, it is not everything. As a treasure hunter works away at his growing gold pile, other treasures often come within reach that

Relics and Gold from Lakes and Sea

Scuba diver exploring floor of Caribbean in search of cannon and other metal objects.—*Photo courtesy Ken White, Sr.*

demand attention. The floor of the Great Lakes is an especially rewarding, little touched place to find things which command high prices in the collector's market.

War Relics Under the Lakes

Among the collectibles which litter the Lake floors are a variety of relics from war years as well as peaceful centuries of trading. As in all the seas, the lakes contain a certain amount of scattered single items, mostly from lost or jettisoned deck cargoes. Locating these objects is largely a matter of luck. To save time and money, treasure hunters will do better to locate wrecks likely to have been loaded with nonperishables which are now of extra value. Here is one: During the War of 1812 the enemy captured a 100-ton schooner named *Ariel* and sank it in Lake Erie about a mile out from the harbor of Buffalo. As a fighting ship, it would be well equipped with small arms, cannon, and other military supplies. This hulk, if it could be found today, would supply a large quantity of the type of relics eagerly sought by museums around the country.

Almost fifty years prior to the loss of the *Ariel,* late in the month of August, 1763, the armed British sloop *Beaver* foundered in eastern Lake Erie. The wreck lies approximately three miles off the beach and fourteen miles south of Buffalo. Although records do not indicate any success for efforts to find the *Beaver,* eventually this wreck will be found and its relics salvaged. It should yield many weapons and much military hardware.

The years 1763 and 1764 were witness to both war and natural disaster on the Lakes. Two near catastrophes occurred in Lake Erie off Rocky River, Ohio. Both were caused by storms and both had their beginnings in the problems of the British with the Indians—Ottawa Chief Pontiac in particular. In the year 1763, a longboat armada, commanded by a British army major named Wilkins was wrecked here. Wilkins' "bateaux" fleet, loaded with supplies and 600 men, was sailing to relieve British troops besieged by Indians at Fort Detroit. The expedition was wrecked on the south shore of Lake Erie, just east of the mouth of Rocky River. Twenty boats, 73 men, and a large quantity of supplies was lost in the disaster. A number of field pieces also disappeared into the surf. Except for a few relics found at random during the years since the fleet came ashore, the wreckage is undoubtedly there yet, covered by sand and silt.

The following year, under almost identical circumstances, the sailing longboat fleet of another British officer met a similar fate. Early in the year 1764, Colonel (later major general) John Bradstreet, in company with forty companies of

Relics and Gold from Lakes and Sea

boatmen, headed for Fort Detroit to put the unruly Indians in their place. A few short months later, Bradstreet, convinced that the Indians would honor the peace treaty he had arranged, was back on Lake Erie with his fleet. It was fall, 1764: storm time.

Bradstreet, his bateaux, and his men were soon dumped into the wind-driven waves west of Rocky River's mouth. The vessels carried gun flints, bayonets, muskets, table silver and Indian trade goods, all of which would have much value today.

A metal detector with a waterproof loop would save time for anybody searching the Rocky River area for relics from the Wilkins and Bradstreet ships. Their dimly remembered misfortune could bring good fortune to a present-day treasure hunter.

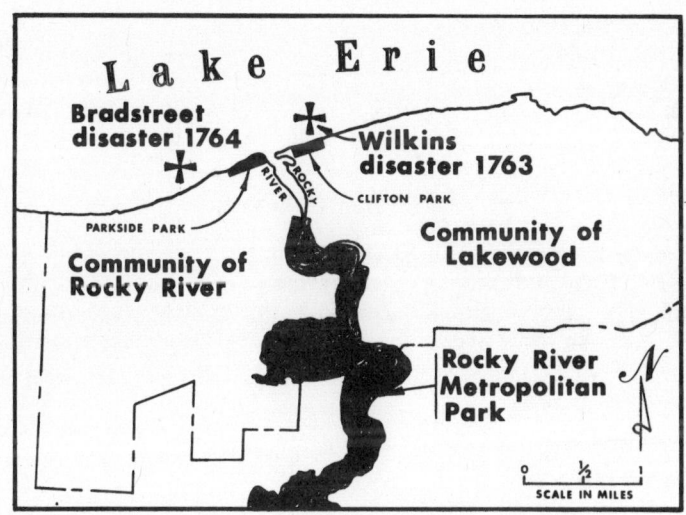

Sites of the 1763 Wilkins and 1764 Bradstreet Disasters

Wreck of the Griffin

Other generals and explorers who had a say in the early formation of this country left tracks which can be picked up today, as witness the adventures of Robert Cavelier, sieur de La Salle. The Great Lakes figured heavily in the adventures and misadventures of La Salle. His career began a long downward slide after the loss of a single vessel, the *Griffin*. This small sailing ship was the first on the Lakes and was to have been put to work as a money maker hauling supplies in and furs out. Unfortunately for La Salle, the ship went down on the first trip.

Somewhere in northern Lake Michigan or Lake Huron, the *Griffin*'s timbers lie still and quiet. If the ship is in deep water, little change will have come to those timbers. A cargo of furs will long have ceased to exist, although a remnant of these may yet cling together in the dark, green depths. But the *Griffin* reportedly also carried a large sum of money in gold coin. To find and recover such a treasure would not only bring personal wealth to the finder, but fame also because of the great historical value of the wreck and relics.

Sunken treasure naturally fires the imagination of adventurers. It is not especially difficult to get within a few hundred feet of incredible riches, though this provides plenty of thrills. The hard part is getting through those last few hundred vertical feet, a task that requires years of planning. But for anyone once infected by the sunken treasure fever, the only cure is actually searching. Fortunately, even small success can serve to cool the fever. It could be a lake, a river, or the shallows of a nearby sea that will give up some treasure.

chapter five

The Lowdown on Metal Detectors— Mystical and Electronic

HAPPINESS in the buried treasure business is a set of instructions which put an X on the place to dig. But most of us are not so well provided for, so we must find another route or give up the hunt.

A marriage of brains and science can uncover more booty than a dozen maps of unknown beginnings. In treasure hunting, science means some kind of electronic metal-locating instrument. One class of treasure finder, however, depends upon mystical forces which nobody clearly understands. A simple test exists which enables anyone to check for sensitivity. It merely requires holding a string between thumb and forefinger.

The Divining Pendulum

For a start, obtain a ten-inch length of heavy silk thread and a small weight. Silk is best but nylon will usually work fine.

Fasten the weight to one end of the line and hold the other end between thumb and forefinger so that the weight hangs free.

This is the divining pendulum, or "pendy," that the ancient Egyptians and Babylonians probably used for exactly the same purposes as it is used today. We don't know if they were any better at using it than we, though there is certainly some room for improvement in the results most people get with this device. But don't be afraid of failure. The divining pendy is worth trying; in fact, it develops the power of concentration.

The pendulum weight itself is not critical, but some materials and shapes seem to work a little better than others. Ivory makes the best pendulum weight; then comes ebony and then the noble metals: gold, silver, and platinum. In a pinch, use a leaden pear-shaped fishline sinker. But first dip it in gold paint. Whatever the material, the best pendulums are pear-shaped, although a perfectly round ball will work well enough.

Size does not make much difference, but a diameter of half an inch at the thickest part and a length of three-quarters of an inch is a practical size. Fastening the silk cord through the eye completes preparations for the test.

Radiesthesia

The exploratory pendulum is one of several devices believed to be controlled in some mysterious manner by the subconscious mind. It responds best to people whose subconscious can break out and send a message by way of the device. This ability is known as radiesthesia, and one either has it or doesn't. Some people, therefore, can make it work and others don't have much success, no matter how hard they try.

Fortunately, equipment for using radiesthesia doesn't cost much and experimenting is easy. In fact, of the aids available to treasure hunting, radiesthesia is the least expensive. Considering its cost, even a small profit from radiesthesia would make it a bargain.

Divining rods, exploratory pendulums, and dip needles are all devices covered by the term radiesthesia. The divining rod, which comes to us from the ancient past, continues to be a popular occult method of searching for hidden gold. Used at first for locating mineral deposits, by the year 1790 it was employed almost entirely to find underground water. Today, although this practice persists, the name has changed to "dowsing."

Gifted treasure hunters still use dip needles and pendulums to locate buried valuables and precious metal deposits. Dip needles are more suited to field work, but the pendulum is said to work anywhere, even hundreds of miles from the actual treasure site.

One thing is certain: none of the radiesthesia devices will so much as wiggle unless held by human hands. The device itself does not possess an all-seeing eye, but rather the human brain. This phenomenon surprises even experts when it comes to performing the unexpected. But, on with the test.

Operating the Pendulum

Pick up the silken cord which has been tied to the pear-shaped weight and hold the upper end between a thumb and forefinger. Right or left hand is unimportant. Use whichever is natural. Simply let the pendulum hang free and steady. After a short period of time, it will begin to swing of its own accord. It may glide back and forth or swing in a circle. The cause for this variance seems to be connected to the sex of the operator. For instance, the pendulum is supposed to swing to and fro over a man's hand; over a woman's hand, it is working correctly if it swings in a circle.

Using the divining pendulum.

Stunts with the Pendulum

Here is a flashy stunt which can be tried after some practice. Place the pendulum over a sealed envelope which holds an unknown personal object clearly owned by either a man or woman. Then see if the pendulum will reveal the sex of the owner.

Another interesting test calls for a standard 12-inch school ruler. The ruler is supposed to polarize the mental powers of the operator in the same fashion as a standard magnet polarizes iron objects. For this test, set the ruler flat on a table or desk. Suspend the pendulum exactly over the 6-inch line (midpoint) by grasping the silk cord as before. If the pendulum is held by a person sensitive to mental magnetism, the pendulum will begin to swing in a direction set by the length of the ruler. Move the string to place the weight over the 0-inch or 12-inch line and the pendulum should stop

The Lowdown on Metal Detectors 75

moving. Move it back to the center and it should begin to swing once again.

A variation of this experiment consists of holding the pendulum directly over the center of a tumbler and about a half-inch above for clearance. Concentrate on the weight and don't be surprised to see it begin to circle the tumbler. It may, in fact, swing in a circle much larger than the glass itself. Be careful to hold your hand rock-steady. Make no effort to swing the pendulum; just concentrate.

Treasure Hunting with the Pendulum

So much for tests. In actual use, the pendulum indicates where on a map the item being searched for is hidden. To find the location of the treasure, move the pendy slowly over the face of the map. When the pendulum reaches the proper spot, the weight will begin circling.

The remaining devices which employ mind power, occult power, or outright magic to locate hidden or lost objects hold less interest than the pendulum. They are also more difficult to construct and operate. Master the pendy first before going on to the more difficult occult detectors.

Electronic Metal Detectors

The electronic metal detector is more complex than the swinging pendulum but requires no special talents for its operation. If you can follow instructions, it's simple. A little practice makes it easy to operate an electronic unit.

Even deaf people can operate certain kinds of electronic metal detector. Very few units fail to perform as expected, and that is to signal the presence of metal at depths up to thirty feet. Metal locators of ordinary design, with the exception of the magnetometer described later in this chapter, do not work at depths greater than thirty feet.

Present-day commercial metal detectors owe their success

to that miniature electronic component called a transistor. Everybody knows about transistors because they go into everything from heart pacers to auto engine ignition systems. In between, transistors can be found in computers, cameras, and conveyors. They are the heartbeat of television, telemetry, and—most important for our purposes—treasure finders.

Most treasure hoards consist of bullion or specie, which in plain language means solid gold bars or spendable cash. Therefore, a metal detector used to signal the presence of precious metal becomes a treasure finder. Whether the target is a chest full of Spanish gold or a single standing Liberty quarter, it is treasure. In either instance, preliminary investigation will narrow the area of search, and the detector will tell exactly where to dig.

Metal locator design has gone through a long period of refinement, as have all other electronic devices. The basic circuits, however, continue in use, just as the basic designs of radios and TV sets continue to be used. There have been breakthroughs in design of component parts, but the functional framework of the electronic circuitry remains unchanged in each type of instrument.

Commercial metal locators come in four types. In order of increasing depth penetration, they are:

1. Beat frequency
2. Induction balance
3. Transmitter-receiver
4. Proton magnetometer

Beat frequency (BF) units excel in detecting small objects at ranges of one to seven inches and large objects like a minnow bucket as far away as two feet. Induction balance and BF units have similar range patterns, with the induction balance type having a slight edge in sensitivity and a greater detection distance. Here the similarity ends. Actual operation of each unit requires separate skills.

The Lowdown on Metal Detectors

The transmitter-receiver instrument does not work on small objects. This unit requires a different type of skill from either of the previous two and is normally used for detection of very deep objects, up to twenty-five or thirty feet.

The ingenious proton magnetometer deserves the name of super detector, and every serious treasure hunter should put it on his want list. This device has absolutely no competition in locating a ferrous mass such as a steel ship. A magnetometer can detect a sunken iron or steel vessel as far away as 1000 feet from its resting place. Smaller iron pieces such as a cannon will produce a magnetometer reading from up to 100 feet away.

The transmitter-receiver unit and the magnetometer are essential to the business of treasure hunting, but beginners should first master the skills needed to use BF and induction balance instruments before going on to the long-range devices.

Beat Frequency

Because a well-designed BF detector speaks in many voices according to what it sees belowground, it helps practiced operators to save time. The varied voices peculiar to the BF unit result from the method used to create the signal. In the beat frequency class of detector, the design is centered around twin radio transmitters, one called the search oscillator, and its identical twin, called the reference oscillator. An electronic circuit designed to detect tiny changes in the search oscillator frequency compares signals from these radio wave generators.

A metallic object placed close to the search loop will cause the expected frequency shift.* When this happens, a place in

---

*In theory, a ferrous metal target (iron or iron alloy) will cause a tone shift in a BF metal detector which is opposite in direction to the tone shift produced by a non-ferrous target (gold, silver, copper, aluminum). Because of the behavior of induced currents, however, such differentiation does not appear in practice, nor can it be effected without an accompanying severe reduction of the instrument's ability to react to the presence of any metal whatsoever. Check carefully the claims of any manufacturer who specifies otherwise.

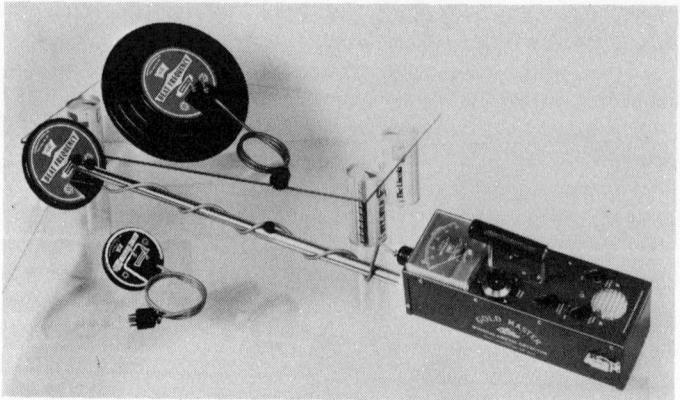

Beat frequency metal locator.

the circuitry called the product detector emits a faint sound. The signal, now an audible frequency, is amplified to hearing level. The amplified sound, or tone, informs the operator of the presence of nearby metal, while the tonality, or timbre, of the sound enables a skilled operator to identify the type of metal in the target.

Signals result from buried metal objects regardless of the overburden of sand, rock, or wood except when the covering consists of heavily mineralized sand or earth. Mineralized soils present problems, although some detector models have controls designed to partly neutralize this effect.

One control incorporated in all BF models allows the operator to adjust the reference oscillator to a frequency just below that of the search oscillator. This small initial frequency shift gives the BF metal detector its great sensitivity and ability to respond differently to various metal targets.

The operation of a BF metal detector depends upon an involved sequence of events which start with the energizing of the search and reference oscillators with a frequency usually somewhere between 100 to 2000 kilohertz. It is common to compromise on 1000 KHZ. To check this frequency, listen to the signal from the detector on an AM radio.

This radio frequency energy is fed to the search loop, but is not usable directly to indicate the presence of metal. It does, however, start a chain reaction which ends as an audible signal in the speaker. The reaction, although a true 1-2-3 sequence, takes place almost instantaneously.

First, the search loop is energized by radio frequency (RF) energy from the search oscillator. (The loop itself comprises a key electrical part of this oscillator.) Second, proximity to metal causes an inductance change. Third, the natural frequency of the search oscillator changes. Fourth, an amplified rising tone comes from the speaker.

The tone-making phenomenon can be illustrated by listening to two people whistling a note somewhere close to standard A. Continue to listen as one of the whistlers slowly raises or lowers the whistle pitch. You should hear a third tone, perhaps varying in volume. A fourth one, although present, will be too low to hear. The technical name for this process is beating, or mixing, to get a beat tone. BF units get their name from this phenomenon. To carry the illustration further, suppose that both whistles sound standard A, or 440 hertz. If one whistler decreases the pitch of his tone exactly 20 HZ, it has dropped to 420 HZ. When this occurs, the beat note will have a frequency of 860 HZ. The mixing, or beating together, of two unlike vibrations creates two additional vibrations: one equal to the sum of the mixing frequencies and one equal to the difference.

If the first whistle sounds at standard A (440 HZ) and the second beats against it at 20 HZ less, or 420, a third whistle sound results at 860, or 440 HZ plus 420 HZ. The fourth tone at 20 HZ, to be heard, would require the listener to have eardrums about 2 feet in diameter. Naturally, such sound goes mostly unheard.

The frequencies used in this illustration are, of course, well within the range of hearing, but metal detectors use nonaudible radio frequency vibrations. While occasionally an oxidized tooth filling will pick them up, no human ear has ever responded to the fantastic ripple of a 1000-KHZ radio wave. Beat frequency *principles,* however, continue to apply. The problem when using radio frequencies is to effect just the right amount of shift to get a sound from nonsound signals of approximately 1000 KHZ (kilocycles).

Converting 1000 KHZ to HZ (cycles) will help us to see what is happening: 1000 times 1000 equals 1,000,000 HZ. Mix this frequency with another of 999,560 HZ, and of the two additional signals which result, one is audible at 440 HZ, as follows: 1,000,000 minus 999,560 equals 440 HZ (standard A on the piano).

At this point, the maze of coils, capacitors, and resistors that are part of every BF metal detector must amplify the 440-HZ tone. Instead of lips puckered to whistle an off-key tone, electrons are pushed by the power of a battery to make a sound all their own. As mentioned before, two dissimilar frequencies mixing, or beating together, make the BF detector work. If the two transmitters operate (oscillate) on the same frequency, no beat sound results at the speaker. Moving the search loop to a position only a few inches from a piece of metal induces, or carries, some of the energy in the search loop into the metal piece. The transmitter automatically adjusts for this loss, but in doing so it changes frequency just enough to cause one of the resulting beat notes to fall into the range of human hearing.

This tone is amplified and fed to the speakers or earphones, and the audible beat note indicates the presence of metal. In practice, this effect causes a rapid change in pitch; and even the timbre, or texture, of the sound changes slightly according to the kind of metal in the target. The variation in pitch capability is extremely wide. Starting at a low rattle or popping noise, the tone of the BF unit can be made to rise until it passes the limit of normal hearing (15,000 HZ).

Search loop size determines the range of the BF instrument. Generally speaking, this detector design employs small loops. The practical 8-inch diameter search loop provides universal coverage, although the BF design has the advantage of adaptability to an unlimited number of loop sizes from one inch in diameter up to a diameter of three feet. Search loop diameters over one foot are uncommon, however. The large-diameter search loop cannot detect small items, but works fine for gallon-sized or larger items up to four feet away. Small-diameter search loops are useless for objects more than a foot away, but excellent for detecting items as small as a single twenty-dollar gold piece.

Signal strength greatly diminishes as the distance to the target increases. Therefore, a distant object, to be sensed by the detector, must be of larger surface area than a target in close proximity to the loop.

Assuming a search loop not less than 7 inches nor more than 12 inches in diameter and average soil conditions, a typical BF instrument* can detect a metal target with a face area of 6.25 square inches or diameter of 2.82 inches at a depth of 4 inches, as the diagram on page 82 shows. At a depth of 24 inches, the target must have a surface area of at least 225 square inches or a diameter of 16.92 inches to be detected.

Search coils for use with BF detectors, when waterproofed, will work as well under water as on land.

Induction Balance

Induction balance locators can also be waterproofed for underwater work, but these units do not usually feature interchangeable search coils. This problem, however, may disappear entirely in the near future. White's Electronics, for one, recently introduced a line of induction balance units with interchangeable loops.

The induction balance metal detector operates, as the

---

*The performance of a quality commercial BF detector will exceed these specifications.

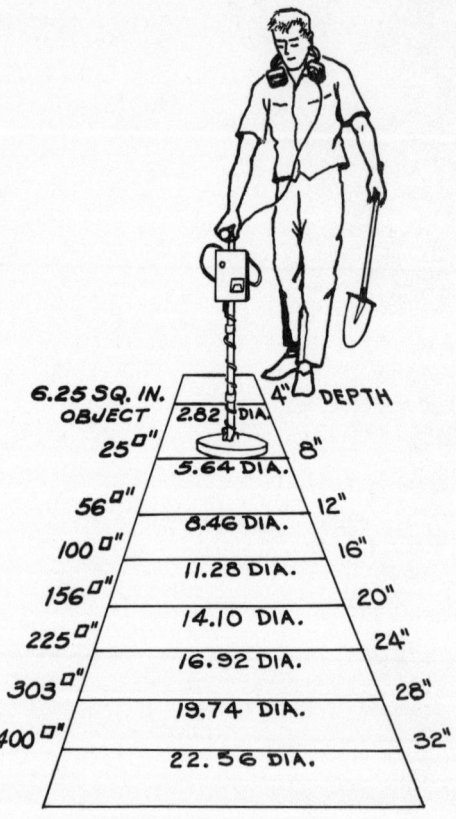

Sensitivity of a typical BF detector.

The Lowdown on Metal Detectors

Induction balance metal detector.

name suggests, by maintaining an electronic balance between two coils. In practice, a pickup coil is installed between two radiating coils. The radiating coils are wound to oppose (balance) each other, and the pickup coil, sandwiched between the two like a piece of bologna between two crackers, cannot pick up a thing. But bringing a metal object close to the coil pack cancels the induction balance, and the third coil picks up the loose energy to produce a signal. This signal is not audible, but further treatment reduces the frequency of the signal to a pitch within range of the human ear. After amplification the weak signal originating in the pickup loop becomes strong enough to operate a pair of earphones, a speaker, or even a meter.

Induction balance metal detectors work well. The depth or earth penetration possible with a quality induction unit on small targets is a genuine thrill. These detectors can recover a single dime or three-cent piece from a depth of ten inches. Don't bury a small coin under ten inches of soil and expect an induction balance unit to find it, however. Such a result is possible only on a coin left in the ground for many years.

Chemically, all of the common coinage metals, except gold, combine over a period of time with the soil they are buried in to a greater or lesser extent. It depends upon soil composition and degree of dampness. The area which is enlarged chemically becomes approximately the same size electrically; therefore, a coin which has been underground for many years will appear larger than life to a metal locator.

Induction balance detectors are especially helpful to tone-deaf persons who still desire to *hear* the signal rather than watch a meter. Tone-deaf ears don't hear changes in pitch. People with this problem cannot, therefore, use the BF metal locator. For them, the best metal locator choice is the induction balance design. It doesn't change tone pitch, but instead emits a sound of varying loudness. This is fortunate for tone-deaf people. An ear which cannot tell a rising tone from one that is descending usually responds quickly to a sound that changes back and forth from loud to soft and soft to loud.

Induction balance and beat frequency units are both available with sensitive meters. The audible signal emitted by all BF and induction balance detectors (except for a few underwater types) is superior to a meter reading as far as convenience is concerned, but in most detectors the meter is no less effective. Because the sense of hearing varies widely among individuals, however, a treasure hunter should choose his type of detector to please his own ears rather than according to the sensitivity or readability of the meter.

Transmitter-Receiver

A beginner should never consider starting out with a radio transmitter-receiver locator. These expensive instruments are totally useless for small items and anything buried less than two feet.

The transmitter-receiver operates on a principle similar to the induction balance detector, but its physical configuration

The Lowdown on Metal Detectors 85

Transmitter-receiver type of metal locator.—*Photo courtesy Tinker & Rasor*

is different. To identify a TR unit, look first for the twin box halves carried on a horizontal beam. There is no other way to operate these instruments. Induction balance and BF devices look quite different. Each is tied to a circular search coil at the end of a slender handle. You will not, however, see a 4-inch diameter search coil on an induction balance unit; it is too small. But BF search coils as tiny as 1-inch diameter are common.

Proton Magnetometer

The proton magnetometer has nothing in common with the three other metal-locating instrument types; it is in a class by itself. This unique instrument raises an alarm at any place on the earth's surface where the earth's magnetic field is warped away from the normal north-south pattern. This occurs only where ferrous (iron) metal or ores turn aside the earth's magnetic flux lines.

The proton magnetometer could not function without the help of a couple of rather awesome forces. One force holds the atom together and the other is the earth's magnetic field.

The technical name of this space age device is proton free-precession magnetometer. It gets its name and usefulness from the effect of a magnetic field on protons in the nuclei of atoms.

Protons are one of the elementary particles which make up the nucleus of the atom. These subatomic bits of matter are said to be spinning about their own centerlines or axes.

No physicist as yet has been able to focus a home movie camera on these infinitesimally small tops, but spinning is about the only way to account for some of the measurable action taking place among the building blocks of the universe, and precession follows.

An ordinary top, if made to tilt while spinning, will precess or, in other words, move in a circle with the point remaining fixed in one position. This is how protons in an atomic nucleus behave. A top is influenced by the earth's gravitational field, while the proton responds to magnetic fields.

Conveniently, the strength of the earth's magnetic field affects protons in a predictable manner. And under certain conditions we can actually listen to the sound made by protons as they dance around their atomic axis. The circling protons emit a tone with the pitch of 2025 HZ, almost five octaves above standard A, well within normal hearing range.

In practice, a fluid rich in hydrogen supplies the protons. Of course liquid hydrogen in the quart size is not readily available, but gasoline, kerosene, and water are obtainable in almost unlimited quantity. Any one of these can furnish hydrogen with its rich supply of protons. Water is preferable for two reasons: safety and availability. The intricate proton free-precession magnetometer does its work with distilled water.

Treasure hunters think of this instrument as a sunken ship finder. If the ship was made of wood, the magnetometer becomes a cannon, cannonball, or anchor locator. These items, like the iron or steel hull of a ship, warp the earth's magnetic field away from its north-south alignment, and passing a proton magnetometer over such a place disturbs its 2025-HZ signal, which begins to burble and flutter like a too-full whistling teakettle. But it is a good sound and music to the treasure hunter's ears.

Manufacturers produce each of the four mentioned detector types for sale. Two of them, the BF detector and proton magnetometer, lend themselves to home construction. They do not require unobtainable parts, but make considerable demands on the assembler. The sure way is to purchase an instrument, even a used one, that bears the name of a reputable manufacturer. Certainly, a metal detector to suit the goal in view should head the beginning treasure hunter's want list.

Prices

Aside from instruments in the $25 to $75 range, which may perform poorly, prices of induction balance and beat frequency detectors are comparable. The prices of quality beat frequency detectors range from about $80 to more than $500. Induction balance detectors sell from about $95 to something under $300.

Several brands of BF detectors have price tags around $25, but although they work or can be made to work, they often have incurable defects. Instability (supersensitivity to jarring or knocking) bedevils all portable instruments, especially the less expensive ones.

The person with only $25 to spend can get around this problem by building his own. Of course, this approach is not for everybody. For those who wish to try this method, however, Chapter 6 tells how to build a detector on a kitchen table, step by step, that will perform as well as any commercial BF instrument in the $100 to $150 class.

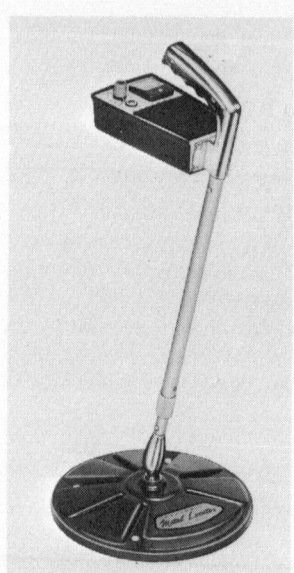

Heath Kit induction balance metal locator.

If your savings account can afford $65, then a Heath Kit detector is one quality answer. Although this kit does not come in BF form, the TR induction balance design shown here performs well. It is easy to assemble and especially sensitive. The Heath Kit detector can locate a dime buried five to six inches deep. In the case of a coin buried underground for many years, this instrument might sense it as deep as nine inches.

Several excellent units incorporating the most needed features sell for slightly under $125. The usual quality instrument in this group offers a minimum of controls and special features. Search loops may or may not be interchangeable, depending on the make, and stability is usually acceptable. Detectors in the $175 price range offer high stability and waterproof search loops as either standard or available items. From this point on, retail costs climb rapidly as gadgetry begins to take over.

Instruments selling for $200 on up boast large-scale meters. Meters can help in certain situations (see Chapter 7), but are not at all essential.

The ultimate in design and quality for a BF instrument should not exceed $350. For those who can spend this kind of money, such a purchase will provide a lot of fun. But so will a $100 detector. It won't be quite so effective as the higher-priced models, but it will work well at the job it was designed to do. And in a short time it will probably recover enough treasure to finance a trade up to something more sophisticated.

Don't waste too much time pondering how much to spend on an instrument. Just remember that it pays to purchase the highest-priced unit you can afford. As prices get higher, so does quality; and to have the use of a quality instrument means less chance of missing a valuable find. Just one miss could well amount to a loss equivalent to the cost of several high-priced metal detectors.

In the better-grade instruments, the buyer's money goes in part for manufacturing know-how and after-sales service. The difference between low- and high-cost metal locators starts with the manufacturing process. Any piece of merchandise, including a metal detector, can be sold for less money by making it in great quantity. This may be the only reason for the lower price of certain brands.

Manufacturers employ two basic approaches to the fabrication and sale of a thousand different articles of merchandise of which the metal detector is only one. One type of manufacturing approach is illustrated by the industrial leader who dominates his particular market because of a policy of continual research and development, or R and D, the industrialists' term. Such effort costs money, but results in goods that usually excel those of a less concerned rival. The higher retail cost of instruments made by these manufacturers arises from the many extra costs of development, testing, new machinery, and service. The detector manufacturer who offers these extras must charge more for his instruments, but he is also selling the latest in engineering and scientific thought.

The other type of manufacturer is known in the trade as an assembler. This fellow doesn't worry about research and development. Whether he is building motors, mukluks, or metal detectors, he makes them with designs scrounged from trade journals or copies from previous models of another builder.

Nevertheless, there are some real bargains available in this category. Do not consider everything that is low in price to be worthless. Sometimes older designs are actually superior, especially in the metal detector field. Designs ten years old and more are being offered for sale. Some of them, in the $25-$75 range, may require additional work to get them going; but others do perform properly and reflect a considerable saving.

Regardless of price, get a metal detector. Remember that even a low-quality detector is superior to none at all.

chapter six

How to Make Your Own Detector

BUILDING a metal detector in your own workshop has many advantages, and none of them need be related to cost savings. But the opportunity to save $100 by making rather than buying an instrument should not be quickly dismissed.

The workshop referred to can be a kitchen table, a card table in the recreation room, or a regulation work bench in a basement shop. Just be sure to follow the assembly plans and instructions exactly as given in the text. Not only will this approach result in a quality instrument always ready to go to work, but it will provide a basis of comparison for the performance of future homemade or purchased detectors.

The electronic instrument described here is a beat frequency metal detector. Most electronic supply houses sell the standard electronic components required to make it. Do not substitute components with electrical values different from those called for. A serious lack of stability and poor sensitivity will result from the use of improper parts. Total cost should not exceed $40. The result will be a quality instrument, well able to compete with commercial instruments in the $150 class.

Construction Methods

To build this detector, a semiminiaturized electronic device to detect the presence of nearby metal objects, the treasure hunter can choose between two construction approaches: hand wiring the chassis and the printed, or etched, circuit board method. An experienced electronic experimenter may prefer to work with the accompanying schematic diagram and make the electrical connections with point-to-point hand wiring. It is a convenient way to make use of material on hand such as common bakelite mounting board and conventional components.

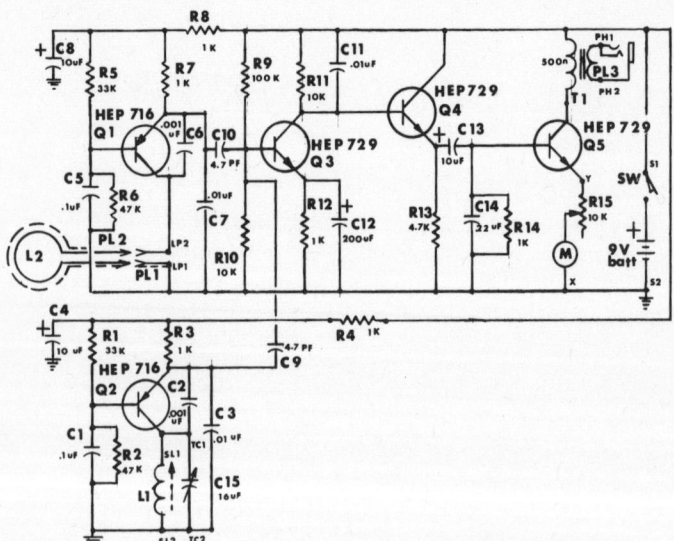

Schematic diagram of beat frequency 5-transistor metal locator described in the text.

The printed circuit board (PC board) presents fewer construction difficulties. Anybody, including first-timers, can use the printed circuit board approach. Moreover, this method offers some definite advantages. Not only does it provide rock-steady stability but the built-in wiring accuracy of a PC board practically eliminates mistakes.

The schematic diagram furnishes information essential to the builder employing the etched circuit board method as well as the hand-wiring buff and experimenter. Consult this diagram to determine the cause of a malfunction such as may occur in any electronic device when component parts become defective through use or mishap. It is necessary to refer to the schematic because the electrical design of the instrument cannot easily be read from the physical layout of the PC board, shown in Figure 2 later in this chapter.

Tools

You will need a few hand tools to build the detector. The average home or car owner's tool kit includes most of these implements. They are as follows:

1. 6-inch, long-nosed pliers (needle-nosed)
2. 6-inch diagonal cutting pliers
3. Screwdriver assortment
4. 25-30-watt pencil-type soldering iron
5. Standard metal-cutting twist drill set (1/16" to ½" diameter)
6. #60 high-speed steel metal-cutting twist drill
7. ¼-inch electric or hand speed drill and chuck
8. Hacksaw with fine-tooth blade
9. Bench vise

Supplies

The tool kit must be supplemented with the following

nonelectronic supplies, obtainable from electronic supply houses:

1. Plain steel wool (not a soap pad)
2. Solder (see Choice of Solder, below)
3. Circuit board etchant for copper (1 pint)
4. Circuit board "resist" enamel in ball-point dispenser
5. Copper-clad (one side only) epoxy glass laminate for printed circuit use (substitute bakelite copper laminate if epoxy glass is not available), finished size 2½" x 4½"
6. Plastic tray, 4" x 5" x 1" deep (see text)
7. Piece carbon paper, 3" x 4½" (1 required)
8. 3-oz. size Dow Corning marine silicone sealant (2 required)
9. 1-oz. size epoxy glue (1 required)
10. Marine plywood 12" x 12" x ⅜" thick (1 required)
11. Soft copper tube, ½" diameter x 2' long (1 required)
12. ¾" diameter x 5' long aluminum electrical conduit (1 required)
13. Bicycle handlebar grip to fit ¾" conduit.
14. Assortment (#4 x 40, #6 x 32, #8 x 24) machine screws and nuts

Items numbered 2, 3, 4, and 5 can be purchased at most large electronic supply houses, or by mail order from Allied Radio Shack, Lafayette Radio Electronics, or Olson Electronics (see addresses under Electronic Parts Supply Houses in the back of the book).

Electronic Parts

In the following list of electronic parts, the lefthand column contains the symbols for the parts as they appear in the wiring diagrams in this chapter.

Symbol	Description
C1, C5	.1-microfarad* disc-type ceramic capacitor
C2, C6	.001 microfarad polystyrene capacitor
C3, C7	.01-microfarad polystyrene capacitor
C4, C8, C13	10-microfarad 15-volt electrolytic capacitor
C9, C10	4.7-picofarad† disc-type ceramic capacitor (critical value)
C11	.01-microfarad disc-type ceramic capacitor
C12	200-microfarad 6-volt electrolytic capacitor
C14	.22-microfarad disc-type ceramic capacitor
C15	16-microfarad variable capacitor (Hammarlund #HFA-15-B)
R1, R5	33,000-ohm‡ ¼-watt carbon resistor (orange-orange-orange)§
R2, R6	47,000-ohm ¼-watt carbon resistor (yellow-violet-orange)

---

*The microfarad is one-millionth of a farad, which is the standard unit of capacitance. It is represented in the schematic diagram above as uF. Capacitive values are stenciled on body of each component.

†The picofarad is one-trillionth of a farad. It is represented in the schematic diagram above by the symbol PF. This unit is also known as the micro-microfarad, but picofarad is now more commonly used.

‡The ohm is the standard unit of resistance. Unit values below 1000 ohms are shown in the schematic diagram above by the symbol Ω. Unit values over 1000 ohms are shown by one or more digits followed by K, which indicates a multiplier of 1000. Thus, 47K in the diagram means 47,000 ohms.

§Resistance values are indicated by colored bands or dots on the resistor body. Refer to the legend of the diagram, How Color Band Patterns Are Used to Signify Resistor Size and Grade. The band closest to one end stands for the first digit of the resistance value. The second band from the end stands for the second digit of the resistance value. The third band indicates whether the foregoing digits must be multiplied by 10, 100, 1000, 10,000, 100,000, 1,000,000, 1/10, or 1/100 to obtain the total resistance value. As can be seen from the legend, such multiplication usually consists of adding the requisite number of zeros to the first and second digits. The fourth colored band indicates manufacturing accuracy (tolerance) of the stated value. Resistors of 20 percent tolerance are less expensive than those of 5 percent tolerance. Resistors of 10 percent tolerance represent a good cost compromise and are adequate for all purposes in this metal detector circuit.

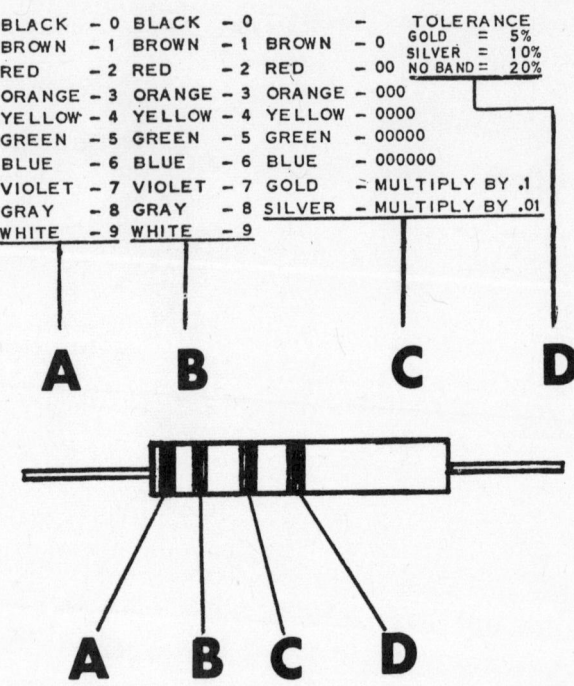

How Color Band Patterns Are Used to Signify Resistor Size and Grade

Symbol	Description
R3, R4, R7, R8, R12, R14	1000-ohm ¼-watt carbon resistor (brown-black-red)
R9	100,000-ohm ¼-watt carbon resistor (brown-black-yellow)
R10, R11	10,000-ohm ¼-watt carbon resistor (brown-black-orange)

Symbol	Description
R13	4700-ohm ¼-watt carbon resistor (yellow-violet-red)
R15	10,000-ohm carbon audio volume control with switch (Lafayette #32E22528)
Q1, Q2	silicon PNP transistor (Motorola #HEP-716)
Q3, Q4, Q5	silicon NPN transistor (Motorola #HEP-729)
L1	.05- to .300-microhenry* powdered iron core variable inductor (Miller #6196)
L2	search loop (refer to text)
T1	500-ohm primary, 8-ohm secondary, 150-milliwatt transistor-type output transformer (Argonne #AR-164)
—	9-volt transistor-type battery (Eveready #246 or equivalent)
—	battery connector-snap-fastener for 9-volt battery ½-inch connector spacing (McGee #BC-9)

Hardware

In the following list of hardware, the lefthand column contains the symbols for the parts which appear in the schematic diagram in this chapter.

Symbol	Quantity	Description
PL1	1	female chassis receptacle (Amphenol #80PC-2F)
PL2	1	male cable plug (Amphenol #80MC-2M)
PL3	1	3-circuit phone jack for phone plug PL4 (Little Jax #12-B)

---

*The microhenry is one-millionth of a henry, which is the unit of inductance.

Symbol	Quantity	Description
M	1	D.C. microammeter, 500 microamps (McGee #23-204) (Olson #ME-101)
—	4	spacers (H.H. Smith #2102 #6 screw x ¾" long.)
—	1	case (Bud aluminum minibox, 7" x 5" x 3", #CU3008A)
—	3	knobs (Lafayette communication receiver knob #99E61053)
—	2	brackets (½" x 1" standard cadmium-plated corner reinforcements)
—	1	wire (100 feet #22 thermoplastic-covered solid hookup wire)
—	1	4 feet #18 2-wire shielded cable (Belden #8422)

Miscellaneous

3/4-inch-wide plastic electronic tape
8-ohm stereo earphones supplied with cord and 3-circuit plug (Allied Radio Shack #KG-801) (Olson #PH-177)

Choice of Solder

Solder, one of the most important supply items, must be chosen with special care. Hardware and large department stores sell several varieties. You must be careful to get the proper one. Ordinary radio-TV solder can do the job, but it has drawbacks. Get printed circuit board solder. It is like no other solder available for electronic work and is usually well identified. Look for these specifications:

How to Make Your Own Detector

1. Rosin multicore
2. 18-gage
3. 60-40 tin-lead alloy

Never, under any circumstances, substitute acid core solder. It will completely ruin an electronic wiring job. Common radio-TV solder comes in a 50-50 tin alloy. Using this material risks overheating transistors and resistors, because 50-50 solder requires a high heat to melt the alloy. The 60-40 alloy, however, melts quickly. Heat greatly hampers successful electronic circuit board construction. Selection of the correct solder alloy will help to minimize heating, and a little care in the soldering process will eliminate the problem completely.

Circuit Board Layout

The etched circuit board is the hub around which everything else grows. Follow directions and you'll be the proud craftsman behind a perfect etching, ready for soldering.

Cut the copper laminate to the exact size shown in Figure 1. Cover it with carbon paper cut to the same size. Make a tracing of the circuit layout from Figure 1 and place this over the carbon sheet. Now retrace the layout so that the pattern appears on the copper laminate in carbon.

Next apply the "resist" enamel from the ball-tip tube. Fill in each area that shows up as black in Figure 1. When this is finished, the copper plate should look exactly like the layout. The only difference will come from the color of the enamel, usually blue. At this point the printed circuit board contains several colored islands surrounded by copper strips. The copper part which remains visible must be removed to create an interconnection pattern for this particular circuit.

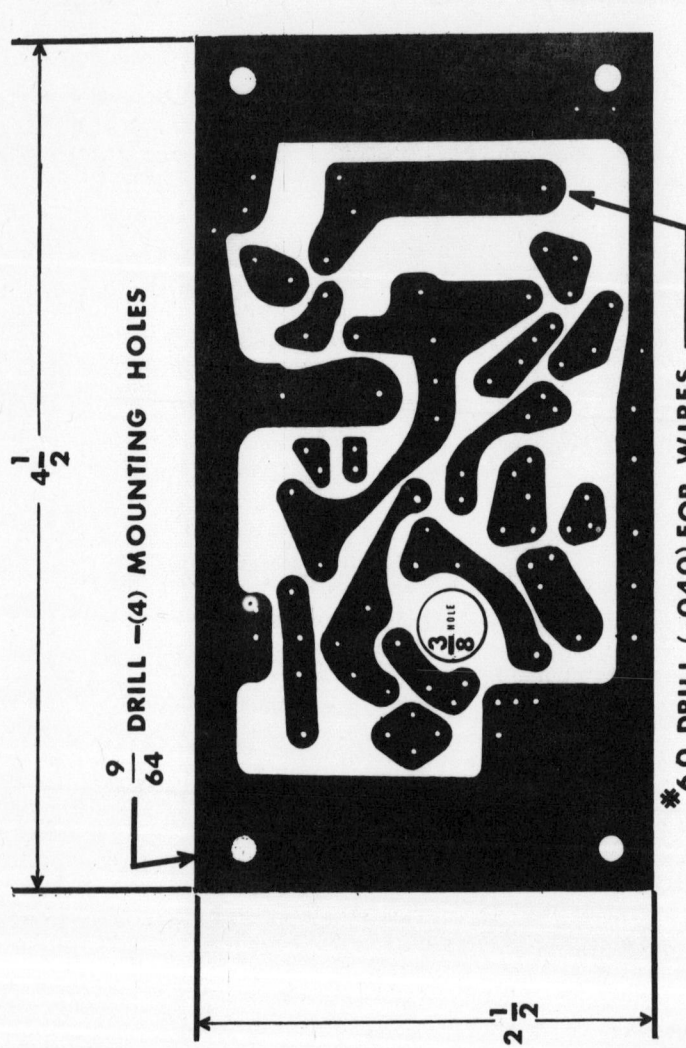

Figure 1

Exact-size view of printed circuit board for metal detector, observed from bottom of board as the finished etching will ap-

Etching

For the next step, employ a liquid-tight, plastic tray. One inch of depth, more or less, will be fine. An old soup bowl can also be pressed into service, but don't use a metal tray and don't use a container that is cracked or chipped. The tray need not be more than an inch larger all around than the copper circuit board.

Pour the contents of the etchant bottle into the tray and place the copper board, face down, into the liquid at a temperature of 70°-90°F. Handle the etchant with care. It will etch you or your clothing even more quickly than the copper.

Leave the circuit board face down for fifteen minutes. At the end of this period, carefully lift the board from the etchant. (Use the long-nosed pliers but rinse them immediately afterwards.) Examine the etching progress by holding the board in front of a light source. The glass or bakelite will be clearly visible when the copper is completely dissolved, because the etched-out areas will transmit light.

When etching is complete, rebottle the etchant and rinse the board and tray in running water until the water runs clear.

Now remove the enamel resist. Clean it off with paint remover, or scratch it away with a plastic or wooden scraper.

When this step is complete, lightly polish the remaining copper strips with plain steel wool (avoid the soap pads found in every kitchen). Polish just enough to brighten the surface.

Drilling

Now, using Figure 1 as a guide, drill all the holes shown. Use the #60 drill for component wire holes. Holes that are too small will make it impossible to assemble the component parts. Holes that are too large will complicate the soldering job. Use a 9/64 drill for the corner mounting holes.

Soldering

The circuit board is now ready for parts; so it's time for another word about soldering. The most common fault in electronic kits put together in home shops is known as a cold solder joint. This serious problem results from hasty work. To avoid this kind of trouble, allow the molten solder to flow onto the copper and around the wire lead. When done properly, the solid pyramid of solder will not bulge outward, but will rather tend to curve inward, and the hardened solder alloy will gleam. A *cold* joint will look dull.

Practice with circuit board scraps and small pieces of wire until you get the correct amount of heat combined with the exact amount of solder.

When you are ready to start soldering, install the parts, one at a time, to the top side of the board (Fig. 2). The wire pigtails will protrude through to the copper underside. Secure each wire with a drop of solder to the copper adjacent to the hole. Double-check polarity of capacitor installation. Match the plus sign appearing on capacitors C4, C8, C12, and C13 with the corresponding plus sign on the circuit board.

When soldering each wire, be careful to avoid heating any part more than necessary, and don't let a solder bridge grow between copper strip conductors. The copper circuit paths run close together and the gaps are easily bridged.

Transistors are especially sensitive to overheating, and those not expert at soldering should use a heat sink when soldering transistors. It's easy to improvise a heat sink from the tip of the long-nosed pliers. Merely grip each wire on the topside with the pliers as soldering takes place on the underside. The heat will be dissipated in the pliers, with very little getting into the transistor.

Pigtails

Install the interconnection wires next (Figs. 2 and 3) at circuit board points LP1-LP2, PH1-PH2, S1-S2, SL1-SL2,

How to Make Your Own Detector

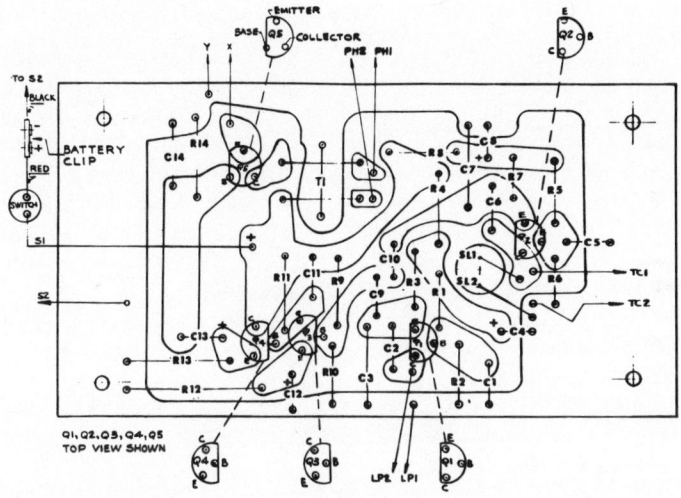

Figure 2

Top view of printed circuit board, showing component parts in position. The copper paths are outlined as though visible from the top to help with part orientation. Transistors are shown in exact location and are also projected outside the board area to help with positioning. Observe the way the flats are located on these epoxy transistors with respect to the PC board. Wires which connect the PC board to case-mounted components are shown with their identifying codes.

TC1-TC2, and X-Y. Start with wires eight inches long and use a different insulation color for each connection. The board is now ready for final assembly.

The Case

Drill the various component holes in the case, as shown in Figure 4. Use the circuit board for a template to locate the four mounting holes and a single hole for the slug-tuned coil stem. Locate the remaining holes from the dimensions in Figure 4. When this step is complete, all is ready for starting final assembly.

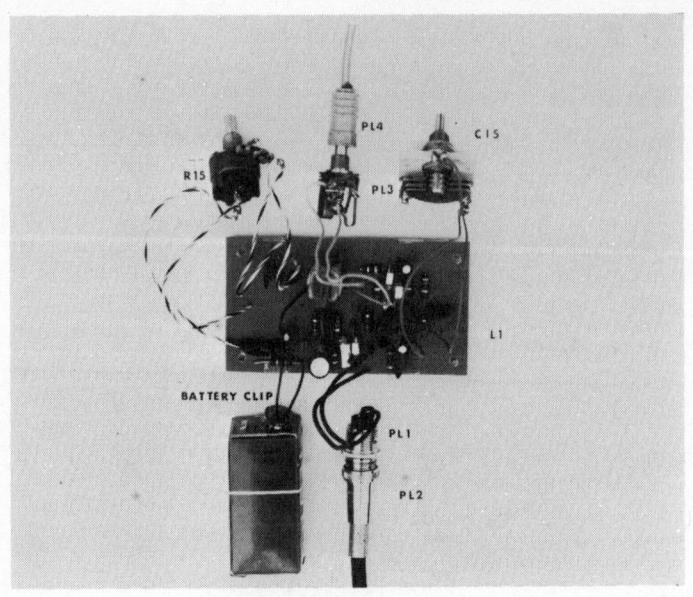

Figure 3

Printed circuit board, showing pigtail wires and attachments.

Earphone Connection

For reasons of economy and comfort, the earphone jack listed under Hardware above is stereo. The earphones specified are also for stereo and they come with a stereo three-circuit plug. A three-circuit jack is required to put these earphones to use without alteration. (Use these same phones to listen to stereo FM, etc.) Because the detector amplifier is single-ended, a shorting link (jumper) is installed on the jack (Fig. 5).

We specify stereo earphones because they have a frequency response much wider than that of the professional radio operator type supplied with commercial detectors.

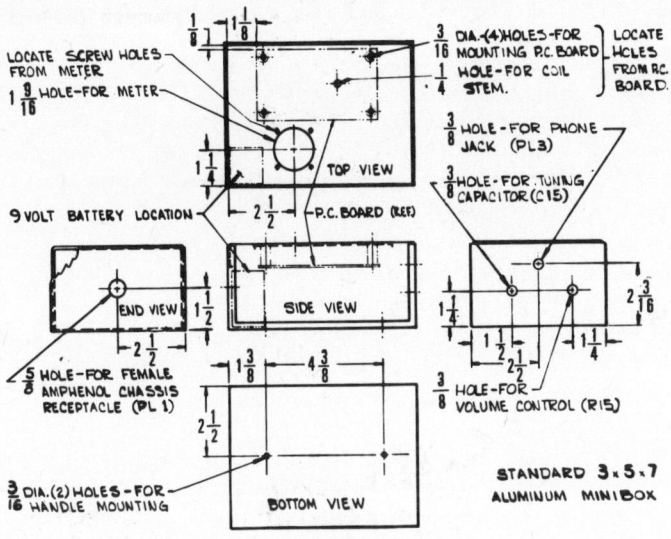

Figure 4

Guide for drilling holes in case.

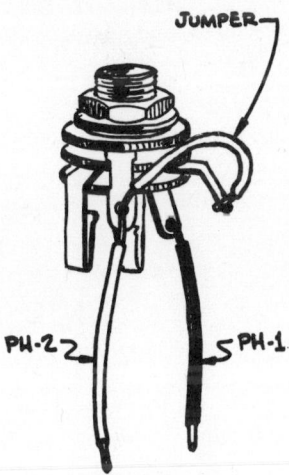

Figure 5

Stereo earphone jack modification detail.

Also, stereo headsets are made to be comfortable, even though worn for several hours. The foam pads help a lot, and the large earcushion contact area provides a remarkably effective acoustic seal. These headsets make it possible to work in the middle of a chivaree and still not hear anything except the moan of the metal detector.

There is one precaution to observe with the stereo headsets. Do not accept substitution of a high-impedance type. The output impedance of the instrument described here is 8 ohms. The earphones must be 8 ohms also.

Again, do not accept high-impedance earphones. Allied Radio sells 8-ohm stereo phones for under $12. Olson Electronics sells a pair for under $10. Send for their catalogs and make your choice.

Hardware Installation

Install the prepared phone jack in the lower case unit and follow through by installing the Amphenol #80PC-2F female chassis receptacle for the search loop plug. Next install the fine-tuning capacitor and the volume control. This completes assembly of the lower unit.

The meter is next to be assembled. It should slip easily into the hole cut into the case upper half. Fasten it securely and proceed to the circuit board.

The circuit board is supported on the case surface by four spacers and secured by four #6 x 32 1-inch-long machine screws. When the circuit board is assembled to the case using the spacers, the 1/16-inch diameter brass stem of the iron core tuning coil will protrude approximately 1/8 inch from the top of the case (see Assembly Detail A). Cement a small plastic washer to the case at this point to protect the brass stem from damage.

This completes assembly of the upper case. Now connect controls and receptacles, located in the lower case, to wires

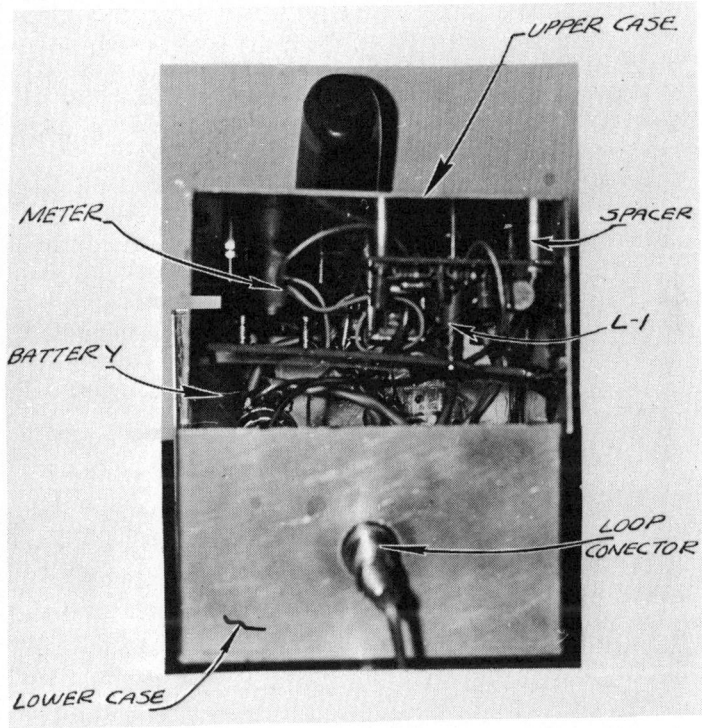

Assembly Detail A

previously assembled to the circuit board. Make the connections as follows:

Battery (9-volt): negative wire from battery connector to point S2 on PC board. Connect positive (+) wire to one switch terminal.

Variable capacitor (C15): connect stator to wire from point TC1. Connect rotor to wire from point TC2.

Slug-tuned coil (L1): one connection to wire from point SL1; one connection to wire from point SL2.

Meter (M): one connection to wire from point X. Add one wire and connect to volume control (R15) center terminal.

Chassis receptacle (PL1): one connection to wire from point LP1; one connection to wire from point LP2.

Phone jack (PL3): one connection to wire from point PH1; one connection to wire from point PH2.

Volume control (R15): one connection to wire from point Y; one connection to wire from meter (M).

Switch (mounted on R15): one connection to wire from point S1; one connection to positive wire from battery connector.

Make the meter connections as shown in Figure 6. If the meter works backward, simply reverse the connections.

The easiest method for a permanent battery installation is

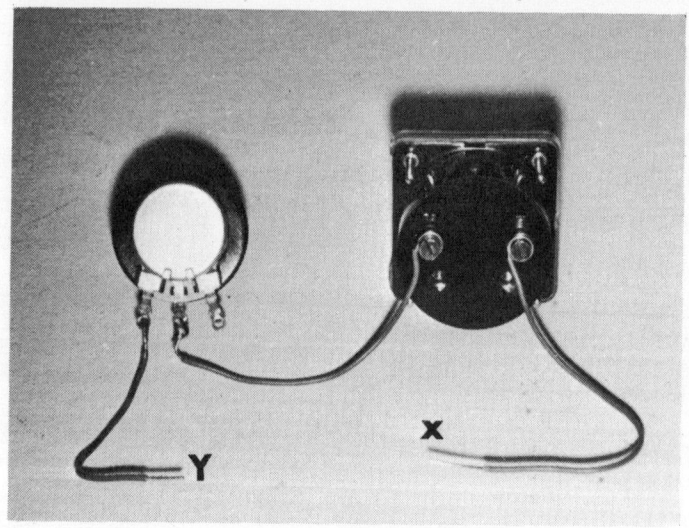

Figure 6

Meter connections.

to simply epoxy it in place. The recommended battery will last about 100 hours, and that's a lot of time in the field. To replace a battery, simply dislodge the old battery with a screwdriver and glue the new one in place.

The control head is now complete and can be bolted to the handle. Be careful of the wires which run all over the interior. Don't accidentally pull one off while attaching the case to the handle. Next comes the search loop. When it is finished, the detector will be complete.

Search Loop

Observing three critically important requirements will ensure successful search loop construction.

1. The correct *length* of wire wound into the coil.
2. The need to securely anchor the coil to prevent the individual wires from moving.
3. The use of a Faraday shield to minimize capacitance coupling with the earth.

None of the remaining construction details are critical. Design can be varied to suit individual needs, but don't ignore the three basic specifications. The following method, however, is quick and certain (Fig. 7).

First, cut the ⅜-inch marine plywood square into an 8-inch diameter circle. Bore a 1-inch hole in the exact center. Next, prepare the copper Faraday shield by bending the 24-inch length of ½-inch *soft* copper tube around the plywood circle. The air gap between the ends of the copper tube is intended. Do not close this gap, as the operation of the loop depends upon it.

After forming the tube into a circle, place it in a vise and split the outside wall for the full length of the tube. Now open the saw cut to form a "C"-shaped section, also the full length of the tube. Lightly burnish the copper with steel wool. Next, slip this "C"-section ring over the plywood disc

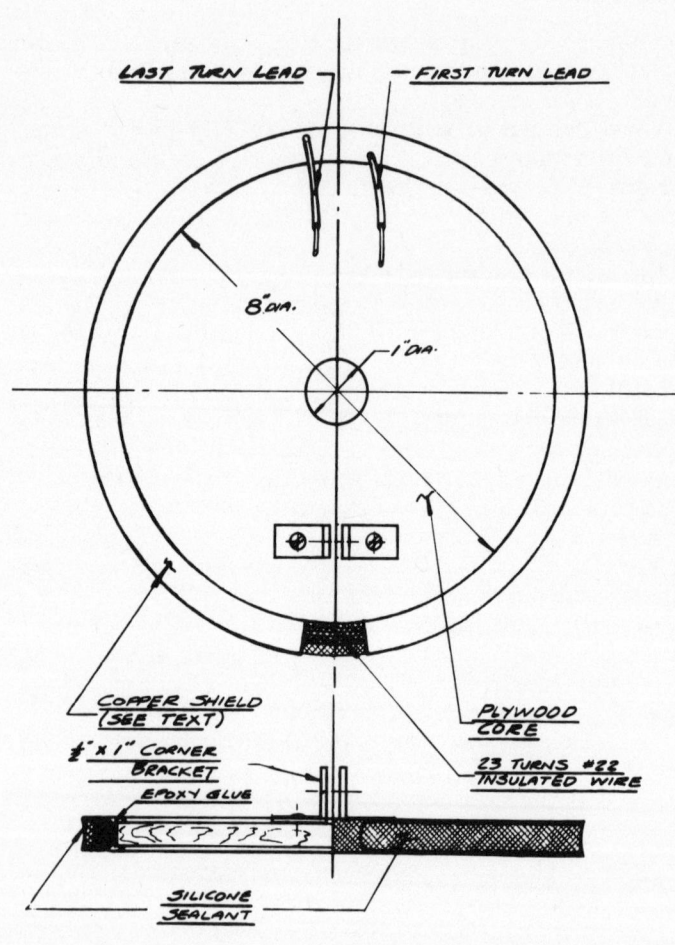

Figure 7
Details of search loop construction.

How to Make Your Own Detector

and, using epoxy glue, secure the ring to the plywood. Allow the epoxy resin time to cure (usually 24 hours) before proceeding to the next step.

When the glue is well set, drill two 1/16-inch diameter holes in the top surface of the copper ring, exactly opposite the gap. Solder a 4-inch length of bare wire ½ inch distant from the holes in the copper ring. The next step is to wind the search coil.

Litz wire is best for radio frequency coil building because it presents the most area for radiation, although its extreme fragility makes soldering difficult. A coil made of Litz wire is the ultimate. Order Belden #8817. Magnet wire is a good second choice, but its sensitivity to abrasion may result in a break in the thin insulation that will prevent the loop from operating. We recommend, instead, #22 thermoplastic-covered hookup wire as the best choice for a first-time attempt at constructing a loop. This wire is Belden #8530.

You will need 48 feet of wire, whatever the kind. Wind the coil clockwise, but first run the free end of the first winding through one of the two 1/16-inch diameter holes in the copper ring. Tape the loose end temporarily to the plywood center disc and proceed to wind twenty-three turns around the copper trough. Use plenty of tension. Keep the windings tight.

Complete the twenty-third turn, clip the wire three inches longer than needed to complete the last turn and run the free wire end through the second 1/16-inch diameter hole in the copper ring. Twist the two free ends together to keep everything tight.

The next step is connecting to the shielded 2-wire cable which plugs into the control head (Belden #8422). First solder the braided shield to the bare wire connected to the copper ring. Next solder the two insulated conductors to the two free ends of the coil. Don't apply sealing material without checking out the unit.

To make the check, attach the handle to the loop (see As-

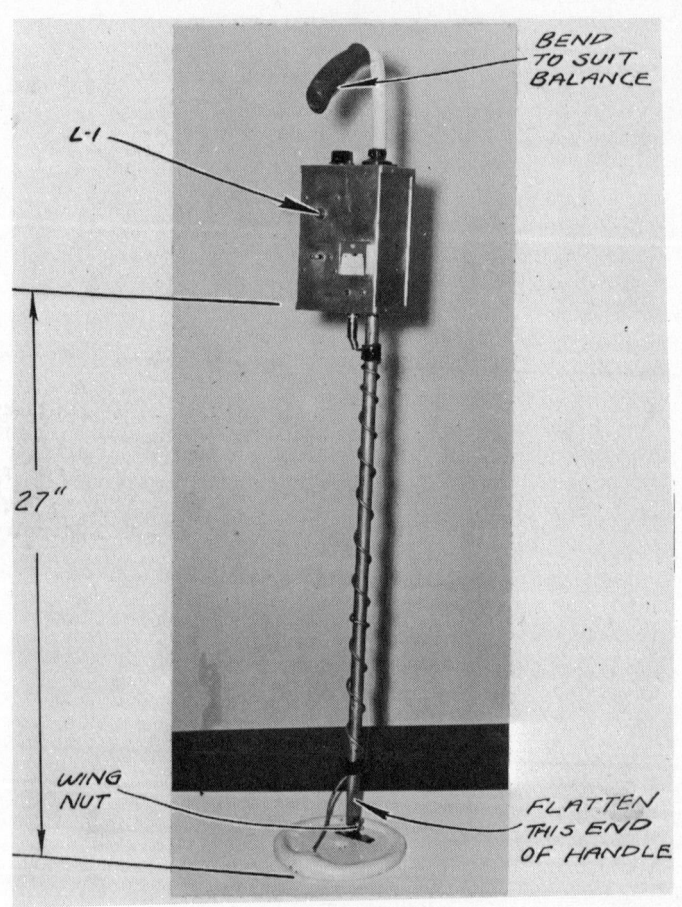

Assembly Detail B

sembly Detail B) and plug in the lead wire at the control head. Plug in the headset and turn the switch on.

Using a small screwdriver, turn the tuning coil slug slowly until a loud tone sounds in the earphones. There will be silence at any other tuning position. Set the tuning capacitor at half-mesh when the coil slug is set in the null or silent half-turn between tone sounds.

The tuning slug can be set to get a rising tone or a descending tone when metal is detected. Be sure to set it for the rising tone. When the instrument is performing properly, use the marine sealant to seal off and immobilize the search coil windings. Don't be skimpy with the sealant. The wires *must* be locked securely. Covering the wire solder joints on the search loop with the same material finishes the job, except for paint.

When the sealant has cured, paint the entire coil with several coats of good *white* outside enamel. The white color will reflect the sun and keep rapid temperature changes from affecting the signal stability. Do not use aluminum or any other metalized paint.

Field Trials

This metal detector is an excellent instrument. A little practice will soon result in a cash return on your investment. Just remember these precautions.

1. The main tuning and fine tuning controls can be set to indicate metal presence with an upswing of sound pitch or a downswing of sound pitch. Always set the controls to produce an upswing of tone pitch. The basic tone should be very low in pitch, but as ears differ in sensitivity, some personal choice is involved here.

2. Keep the search loop close to the ground. This will put a maximum amount of radio frequency energy into the search

area. A large air gap between the earth and the search loop wastes the signal radiating from the search coil.

3. When you prefer not to wear the earphones over your ears, simply carry them around the neck and turn up the volume. The low-impedance stereo phones employ small speakers as reproducers and eliminate the need for installing a separate speaker in the case.

4. When using the meter, set the needle at midscale or lower. Keep your eyes fixed on it while slowly scanning the search area.

Troubleshooting

Following instructions should eliminate any difficulty in getting this project to operate. There are, however, some problems which can occur, as with all electronic devices.

The cold solder joint causes lots of trouble. The only cure for this defect is resoldering.

Check for wrong part installation, reversed negative and positive orientation of capacitors, and check resistor installation. It is possible to transpose the color band arrangement in your mind and thus misplace one of these parts.

Make certain that all interconnection wires are installed and be certain of battery voltage!

chapter seven

Surefire Ways
To Treasure-Hunting Success

LET'S assume that you have bought, begged, built, or borrowed the best available beat frequency metal locator and can't wait to get started on the first treasure hunt. You have to decide whether to go after sunken or buried riches.

Whether the goal is buried or sunken treasure, it takes more than a few obstacles to slow a real treasure hunter. Obviously, however, a search for underwater riches requires a treasure hunter to wear special equipment merely to survive. And, of course, as affected by the weather, buried treasure has it all over the sunken variety. Except for a few days of storm each year, rain, wind, cold, or heat will not interfere with the hunt. Another advantage of buried treasure is its inexhaustible variety. Even without considering pirate loot, in a lifetime it would be impossible to check out all the buried treasure possibilities still awaiting recovery.

Although any treasure hunter can narrow his area of

search by employing the methodical research methods discussed in Chapter 2, the random search of likely places produces many thrills. There is simply no telling what the next item to be found will be. Besides finger rings and earrings, tie clasps, pens, fancy cigarette lighters, watches large and small, religious medals, bracelets, and an unbelievable number and assortment of small pocketknives (the last-named item is often found buried in the sand on public beaches) are apt to turn up.

Using a Detector Effectively

Whatever your choice of detector, read the manufacturer's instructions carefully. This is important. All control units differ slightly from one another and you must understand exactly how to operate *your* instrument in order to get the best results from it.

Control Position

To be sure of not missing anything, always operate any BF instrument in a control position that produces the lowest audible tone possible. With certain types, this will actually not be a tone at all, but rather a rattle somewhat like a plastic card held against the spokes of a rotating bicycle wheel. Also, always set the controls to give a rising tone or faster rattle when a metal target comes into the search loop area. If the controls are set to produce a descending tone or slower rattle over the target, you may go right past a valuable ring or coin because the descending sound falls quickly past the point of audibility. By contrast, the rising sound can range from 50 to over 10,000 Hertz and remain audible right to the top.

Assuring Battery Performance

Top performance of any metal detector depends on battery

condition. Transistors have lengthened battery life. Older vacuum tube instruments—and there are a few still around—use up batteries at a fantastic rate. Older units have other drawbacks, too. The cost and weight of their high-voltage batteries rule out their use by anybody except professionals.

Fortunately, transistors ended the exclusive ways of the professional treasure hunter. The arm-breaking locator of ten years ago is now the 5-pound or less wonder of lightness. Transistor-driven detectors use batteries which last up to 100 hours of use, and the 9-volt battery commonly used in metal detectors is available as easily as photographic film and flashbulbs. But don't let your guard down simply because gas stations and drugstores sell batteries. *Carry a spare or two.* If there is any doubt about the energy remaining in a battery, *throw it away*.

Although some manufacturers claim 100 to 200 hours of battery life, batteries rarely maintain peak voltage for more than 100 hours. In calculating the life of a battery, be sure to take into account the length of time it has been on the shelf. One hundred hours is a safe maximum for a detector with earphone only, 75 hours if it has a meter or loudspeaker, and 50 hours if it has both. Retire a battery at the end of 90 days whether the detector has been used or not unless it is particularly expensive. In this case, test the battery at least every 90 days. You can use batteries after they have been retired from detector use in a transistor radio or other device where peak voltage is not so critical. Each detector devours batteries at a different rate, so some testing is advised.

Keep those batteries fresh! Allowing batteries to remain in the instrument through a winter or a long period of time will weaken them beyond repair.

A metal detector will not operate properly on below normal voltage from the power supply, nor can it do its best on the small #1604 9-volt cell in common use for pocket radios. While this battery can pinch hit for short periods, when there is none other available, it simply does not pack the reserve needed to properly energize the radio transmitters in all metal detectors.

Batteries sold at cut-rate prices may work in flashlights, but don't put them in a metal locator. Voltage output is not at all reliable and the very real possibility of chemical leak and spillage exists. Use a top-grade brand name battery. They cost only slightly more.

Ordinary "D" cells, "C" cells, and penlight "AA" cells are likely to leak if they happen to discharge rapidly. This won't happen often, but shorted wiring is always possible and a short circuit will cause this undesirable rapid discharge of the batteries. Inspect the battery case often; it takes but a minute.

Give any electronic metal detector tender, loving care. No matter how costly or inexpensive the instrument may be, it cannot be replaced except by another unit. Even when price presents no problem, you may not be able to afford the *time* it takes to get a new one. None of these instruments can stand unreasonably rough handling.

Technique

The next item to check off is technique. Expect to spend quite a number of hours in actual field work to develop skill. You must learn to identify the peculiar sound produced by a bottle cap, a coin, a ring top, or a piece of aluminum foil. Aluminum foil causes an especially distinctive sound. Its telltale harshness is easy to recognize, and so are the more subtle characteristics of other metals.

Practice with your metal detector to determine the kind of response it will give under changing conditions and with the various objects likely to be found in the usual search areas. To get an approximation of this reaction, bury samples of these objects at varying depths. Concentrate on the type of signal caused by small and deeply buried targets; you can't afford to miss a single thing.

Effect of Corrosion on Detection Depth

Treasure hunters looking for buried coins are helped by the chemical interaction of the coins and soil. Depending upon the chemical composition of the soil, and moisture, a buried coin grows in electrical size in proportion to the amount of oxidation of the coin metal. If the soil adjacent to a buried coin becomes saturated with metallic salts from the coin metal, the salts add electrically to the size of the coin, which can be detected at a depth greater than a coin not affected by corrosion.

This effect sometimes explains what happens when a signal disappears after a treasure hunter disturbs the soil. If the prober pushes a deeply buried target from its envelope of electrically active chemicals, it may fall too deep to register, being suddenly electrically smaller. The detector operator might think he is receiving a false signal of some sort. If this happens to you, screen every trowelful of dirt down to ten inches in depth. Otherwise you could overlook a fine ring or long-buried rare coin.

Even instruments priced at $600 cannot detect objects buried beyond a certain depth. When the separation between the search head and the metal target gets past the point at which the reflected signal from the object bucks the main signal, then contact is lost. BF and TR detectors *see* the target in terms of surface area presented to the *plane* of the radiating surface. This can become a problem when the target lies in a plane perpendicular to the search loop. For instance, coins frequently lodge on edge when they are lost in sand. The prober must listen very attentively to hear the slight change in detector pitch or intensity which occurs as the search loop passes over such a target. Quality instruments minimize these problems.

When to Use Meters

Meters can be helpful, not only for treasure hunters who

are deaf or hard of hearing, but for those with normal hearing. A meter needle can register tiny inductance changes too small for the average ear to detect. A meter is invaluable when the earphones transmit only a slight flutter of sound. Such a barely audible tone change usually indicates one of three possibilities: a coin on edge, a large coin buried deep (12 inches or more), or a small coin at the extreme edge of detectability (6-9 inches). But don't be surprised if a chase after one of these spooky signals produces nothing more than the spent brass casing of a .22 short pistol round. These pests turn up everywhere.

For those with normal hearing, watching a meter takes second place to listening for a signal, despite the former's special advantages. Underwater treasure hunters working with full scuba diving gear and pressure-sealed one-unit electronic locators find that meters, although necessary for underwater work, present problems. Swimming along the bottom beneath 30-60 feet or more of water with one's eyes glued on the indicator needle of a 4- or 5-inch meter can be quite eerie, especially in murky water. A diver can easily miss an outboard motor or a camera if he looks upward, down, or backward when the needle flips. The ear far excels the eye in interpreting the message of a metal detector.

In the course of a search sweep across bumpy, uneven land, watching a meter can cause falls. Sooner or later, it will happen. Take your meter to the beach. It won't cause complete failure, but using it exclusively will cut results by half.

Marking Hot Spots

As you begin work in the field, adopt the professional habits that will pay off with many valuable finds. For instance, mark each spot that gets a strong reaction from the detector with a large flour-filled salt shaker or a soft plastic detergent bottle also filled with flour. When there is a strong reading, squeeze off a shot of flour over the spot and keep right on scanning. This approach will furnish an idea where the concentrations are. Use your judgment regarding the size of the square or rectangle under search; a half an hour of scanning can make for as much as an hour of digging.

Even worthless items can be a help in deciding where to dig. As you search for treasures, a detector will locate ordinary soft drink bottle caps more than anything else. Trash such as this would be worthless except for one thing: the amount of rust and depth of burial tells whether or not somebody else has searched that particular spot. Bottle caps that are rotten and covered with several inches of earth could mean that you are first on the scene and should give the area a thorough check.

Digging Equipment, Sifters, and Containers

When the time comes to dig, it pays to have good hand tools, probes, screens, and containers. First the digging group: shovels. No small digging tool anywhere can beat an army trenching shovel. You can buy these shovels in army surplus stores, although cut-rate sporting goods stores often sell usable copies. The real article, however, is made of better steel than the usual copy and can withstand more abuse. The best model has a folding blade. In the right-angle locked position this shovel makes an excellent chopping tool. Back up the shovel with a small garden trowel. Get one with a smooth handle, no bumps or knobs.

For serious excavation work, the army-style trenching shovel works best. But coin hunters usually work in sand, in water, or on sod. This type of operation requires a sifter and a small shovel or trowel. Any treasure hunter can make an excellent sifter from an ordinary French-fry basket by bending the handle to improve the grip. Reinforcing the handle with an angle bracket (sold in hardware stores for

122   Introduction to Treasure Hunting

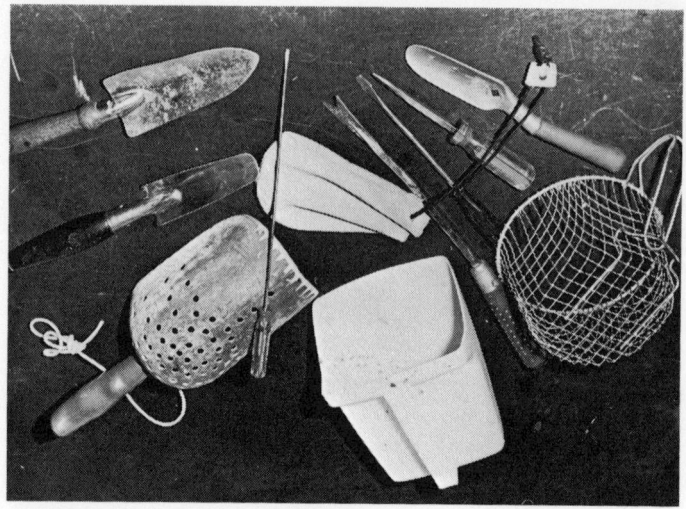

Tools for the dig.

supporting shelves) will improve its structural strength. You can also put together another heavier type from 3-inch pine boards and coarse wire screen. Each has its special uses. A hand-held scoop screen is ideal for use while walking slowly along a sandy beach or play area. The box sifter works best in a limited area or near a handy water supply.

Coin hunters need a secure and quickly accessible place to carry dirty coins as they retrieve them from the ground. Pockets, although the customary place to keep loose change, will not do. Bending, stooping, and sitting tend to spill coins from pockets faster than you can keep them filled. A bag slung over the shoulder or from a belt around the waist eliminates this problem. A large chamois marble bag is an ideal choice. If the dime-store marble bags are too small, look for one of the girls' leather pouch purses which come in all sizes. Simply cut the decorations off.

Although screwdrivers do not work in sand, treasure hunters need two types of these implements for searching various types of terrain. For coin hunting around grassy areas, choose a long, slender screwdriver with a shank 3/16 inch in diameter and 10 inches long. This small screwdriver has no equal for penetrating sod. For probing in clay such as that found in schoolyards or around hard-packed play areas, use a large screwdriver with a 3/8-inch shank and 8 inches long.

Gear for Working in Water

Searching for coins and rings under water at a beach requires special equipment. For this, take along waders. Walking around barefoot, up to your knees in water, can get mighty cold after a couple of hours. Waders will keep the cold out. Wearing a pair of ordinary wool socks inside the waders will make it possible to keep going long after the barefoot daredevils have quit and gone home.

Shallow-water work also requires a floating sieve. This is nothing more than a bucket with holes in it, but it must float. The sifting action does not differ from sifting treasures from beach sand, except that in the water one hand must always hold the detector and the other hand must operate a shovel. Obviously the sifter has to operate automatically. You can't buy this device, but it is really quite simple to make.

Obtain a minnow pail, new or used. You will need the inside part, the one with the holes in it. Also obtain a new or used inner tube for an 8.00 x 12 trailer tire. If the minnow pail has no holes in the bottom, put some in. Do not make the holes larger than ¼ inch, but drill a lot of them. Next inflate the tube and slip it over the pail from the bottom. A common minnow bucket will fit the inside of the tube exactly.

With the tube against the top flange of the bucket, put it to the test. Tie a short rope to the tube. Toss the assembly into water at least a foot deep. The pail should fill with water at once, but the inflated collar will keep it afloat.

Test the action by loading the pail with a shovel of sand,

Floating sieve made from a minnow pail.

gravel, or soil, whatever is handy. Now move the sifter through the water. After a few feet of travel, the sand should be gone. The sieve traps the collectibles from treasure-laden sand or gravel, so that you can pick them out with ease.

While working in water you will be too busy to pay attention to the progress of the search. A previously untouched swimming beach may produce a signal in the detector for every two feet of scan, and as many as half the signals will result in a ring, coin, or other valuable item appearing in the bucket. In cleaning an area thoroughly, do not linger over each find. Save this fun for later.

By now, you may think that a pack horse or a truck will be required to haul the dig-and-search apparatus. But in practical terms, you will need only a portion of your special tool collection on any one particular search. Fortunately, planning each trip in advance makes it possible to travel light. If there is any one secret of overall success, it is planning.

Staying Comfortable

Besides tools that help in moving sand, rock, or earth, any item that helps to keep one comfortable or safe, or increases the searcher's efficiency in the field, qualifies as a tool. Put rugged shoes at the top of the list. Loafers are all right for lounging, but don't put them to a five- or six-hour test in sand, or up and down gravelly hillsides. Hiking boots have no rivals for all-purpose field work, but inexpensive leather work-type shoes will do fine for anything except mountain climbing.

Never leave on a field trip without insect repellent. A tired, wet, dirty, footsore, or overheated treasure hunter may *feel* like quitting, but one attacked by insects will be certain to quit. A small cannister of repellent foam will fit a shirt pocket and last for several outings. It will effectively stop insects from feeding on ankles, neck, and wrists.

Personal choice and the temperature and terrain to be encountered in the field dictate the selection of all other items of clothing and accessories. Some people like sunglasses; others can't be bothered. It is the same with hats, although those staying in the sun most of the day should wear a head cover of some kind.

Safety Precautions

Treasure hunters who know their business always look out for their own and others' safety as well as comfort. This could mean a slight delay before entering a building, cave, or other structure. Be careful in old buildings. No treasure is worth getting injured. Even if floors and walls appear safe, tread cautiously.

Safety could mean returning for a left-behind compass before entering a wooded area. It could mean taking a moment to leave a note spelling out your travel plan for the day. It could mean not reaching into dark holes without first exploring with a rod or stick.

Pocketknives are the only dangerous items which you are likely to find. Occasionally, however, live ammunition will also appear in the basket. *Don't throw it away*. Even very old ammunition can be dangerous; so handle it with respect. If you find live ammunition and do not wish to keep it, give it to a ranger or policeman.

Be professional in every move. It could mean that you will live to add to the most valuable treasure of all—your life.

Avoiding Crowds

Being professional also entails achieving a certain amount of privacy during prospecting operations. Professionals and advanced amateurs shun publicity and seldom, if ever, appear in news of the day. These tight-lipped modern argonauts know the way people are about money, and take precautions to avoid public notice.

Beginning treasure hunters should copy the actions of experienced people and do nothing at any time to attract unnecessary attention. The problem here is to make proper use of the metal detector without getting yourself detected. Shun people detectors in the person of small boys, elderly ladies and gentlemen, and dog walkers. You can do it. Merely get up with the birds. And truthfully, daybreak is the best of all times to start on a treasure hunt. You may come across a few

Surefire Ways to Treasure-Hunting Success

scattered wanderers pretending to be fishermen or steely-eyed early birds fooling around with golf clubs. But these are mostly gentle creatures programed to do only one thing. They won't even notice your presence. Beach, playground, and concession stand will be empty, except possibly for other treasure hunters. But they will be too busy to get in your way.

Weather can also help in achieving privacy. Treasure hunters have the reputation of being weatherproof. They seem to thrive on conditions that keep everybody else under cover or huddled up to the fireplace. Of course, nobody in his right mind is likely to slosh around the countryside during a hurricane or high-pressure electrical storm. There is, however, no better time of year to go digging for buried riches than spring and fall in the North and during the wet seasons in other sections of the country. A nice drizzle offers great privacy and secrecy.

In spite of all precautions, however, spectators will probably turn up during some of your treasure-hunting expeditions. Every group of onlookers will include at least one small boy who thinks you are a spy and threatens to call a policeman. Of course, there is no need to worry if he carries out his threat, but remember, the fewer the delays the better your chances will be to complete your search quickly and skillfully.

Here is one usually successful way to deal with the small boy problem. Get the message across that because of the earphones, you cannot hear a word that he says. But first mention, with a confidential smile, that you are looking for pirate loot. This is no lie, but a perfectly correct answer. Treasure hunters are *always* looking for pirate hoards!

Although we have stressed the need for privacy, sometimes the natural curiosity evoked by metal-locating equipment can be helpful, if your primary aim is making new friends and acquaintances rather than serious treasure hunting. In such a case, simply tote your trusty electronic detector to a beach or park any time during the vacation months. Avoid morning and evening hours. Plan to begin working at high noon or shortly after. You will get more attention in ten minutes than in a year of normal beach activity. There will be many interesting and friendly folk to meet, and you will be amazed at the variety of questions.

chapter eight

Finding, Cleaning, and Selling Coins

NO wonder coins present such a tempting target to treasure hunters. They are hiding everywhere, here and there about the country, scattered in singles, pairs, and clumps—in sand, soil, and clay; on the bottom of lakes, rivers, and ponds; behind fireplace stones, and under building corners. Every day treasure hunters with metal detectors find coins that exceed their face value, some by as much as 100 times.

How Deep Coins Are Buried

Fortunately, few coins are buried deep enough to escape detection by an electronic metal locator, except where filldirt covers them or their original owners purposely buried them at considerable depth. With these exceptions, a metal detector will sense every buried coin, even those resting on edge. Single coins lost for thirty years and more around parks

Finding, Cleaning, and Selling Coins

How to Search Abandoned Buildings with Metal Detectors

Top photo on opposite page shows detector loop being passed over window casing. Small sums of money are often hidden under loosened boards in window frames for quick accessibility. Bottom photo on opposite page shows detector search of building foundation. Bulky items such as jars of coins are often concealed behind loose stones or blocks or at the corners of a foundation. It is usually safer to conduct search from the outside, as photo shows. Photo at left above shows instrument checking out the top of a door casing, always a favorite hiding place. Photo at right above shows the detector loop on the hot spot for staircases, the bottom step. Sometimes hollow railings are filled with coins, but more often steps are used for hiding money, jewels, and guns.

and similar places seldom go deeper than five inches into the earth. In the North, where frost works the ground, coins lost thirty years may stabilize around two inches under the surface according to the type of soil.

Spectacular Coin Finds

Treasure hunters who are just starting out can profit from the successful experiences of old hands. Professional treasure hunter Gene Ballinger tells a story about a friend who was exploring a partially burned out house in Michigan's Upper Peninsula during August of 1969, when he got a strong reaction on his detector. It came from the lintel area of a door frame. The signals turned out to be four leather pouches filled with dimes: 397 of them, all dated prior to 1902; silver dollars: 219 of these dandies, all dated prior to 1922; and 488 twenty-dollar double eagles, all dated prior to 1900. Of course, this fellow did a lot of searching before chancing across such a hoard of coins, but he could have found it on his first try.

Ted Baxter, publisher of a magazine for treasure hunters, thought he would give an exhibition of scientific treasure hunting to an interested buddy, Frank Whitney. The demonstration had spectacular results. This pair of Sunday afternoon treasure hunters found a cache of 300 ancient rare coins. Luck? Certainly, except for one ingredient which these success stories have in common: professional treasure hunters obviously know where to look, and you, too, can make use of the same knowledge.

Coin Hot Spots

Search around fairgrounds, playgrounds, abandoned circus grounds, old amusement parks, boardwalks, and public beaches. Wherever you go, look for signs of long-time human habitation; the longer people have gathered in a place, the better the chances to find something really valuable.

Playgrounds

Don't waste time on areas which do not show signs of human use, such as isolated beaches. Concentrate heavily on well-frequented places. Check out playground swings in schoolyards or at county parks. Unless somebody else gets there first, you simply can't miss. Swings are practically guaranteed sources of small treasures. And if somebody else does clean out a playground or a beach area before you arrive, cheer up. It will be recharged in a few weeks. In some spots the pressure of public use recharges the ground *every day*.

Beaches

Learn to think in terms of situations which cause people to lose money or hide it. For instance, picture the activities of persons using but not dressed for the beach. These casual visitors love to recline on grass which borders the sand. As they watch the antics of swimmers, coins fall from pockets, rings from fingers—each to slip out of sight in the turf. Your metal locator will know where they are. Use it to scan the first four or five feet of grass adjoining every accessible beach.

Don't overlook park benches and other beach furniture. This equipment is most always of open construction, and small items from pockets as well as loosely fitting rings often fall through the openings to be covered by sand, grass, or soil.

Volleyball and Handball Courts

Lost ring and coin hot spots also occur near volleyball or handball courts. The sand around volleyball nets often raised at one end of a beach sometimes hides a complete treasure trove. The abundance of lost items, a little known by-product of volleyball, results from the jumping activity of the game.

Also, keys turn up surprisingly often under the net. People who stuff keys carelessly into a pants or jacket pocket not only lose them on volleyball courts, but also at picnic sites and playgrounds. In a short time, a metal locator can find enough keys to fill a display board exhibiting all types. And occasionally, the treasure hunter with electronic equipment can help the person who is searching on hands and knees for a lost car key.

Parks

Smart treasure hunters never overlook parks when they go coin hunting, or coin shooting. Many popular activities in parks have left behind treasures in lost coins—band concerts, for instance. Fifty years ago, summer weekends were not complete without Sunday evening band concerts in village or city parks. The larger the park the more people got together. An audience could be totally carried away by a triple-tongue tuba cadenza, and this would call for a token of appreciation. The practical method for getting it done was to pass a hat around. During the scramble to sort out the thinnest dimes, a few coins would fall into the grass and be lost forever. Well, not quite forever, for if treasure hunters in the know can find those old parks, they will discover those lost dimes, nickels, and occasional quarters.

Areas near concession stands in parks are also likely hot spots. During the summer of 1969 we were coin shooting a disused path that at one time connected a concession stand with a state park playground. It started as an ordinary field trip with pennies, nickels, and bottle caps being pried out of the clay and sod. At one point an odd signal continued sounding in the speaker even after we removed a 1936 nickel and deepened the hole by another four inches. Again the hole brought a definite but faint flutter of sound from the detector as the search loop passed over the area.

The clay, baked hard under the summer sun, was pretty tough to excavate with a small trowel, and we almost decided to forget it. But something about that flutter whetted our curiosity. We kept on digging until the hole was almost a foot deep. At the bottom we found a handful of change, all silver and not one piece newer than 1928. It was easy to guess what happened to put a handful of coins in that particular spot. The path dipped quite low at this point. At some time in the past, a puddle had probably existed where now coarse grass grew in the yellow clay. A plank may have bridged the low spot, and somebody fell off, or in. Anyway, the stumbler apparently emptied a pocketful of change into the mud, and it remained in the same place for at least forty years. The coins were in good condition and worth considerably more than face.

Our windfall on this obscure footpath resulted from a well-planned conversation about the old days. It was part of a standard plan to learn about a new area as soon as possible after arrival. This time, our *modus operandi* involved an hour or so of pleasant listening to a long-time resident of the area. As he reminisced about the days of his youth, he responded to our interested questioning. Eventually, the elderly gentleman mentioned the long forgotten pathway. We thought it would be worth a couple of hours of attention. It was.

Always seek out people whose memory bank contains much otherwise forgotten important local history. We happened to be vacationing 600 miles from home, but knew from past experience that each new place holds a variety of excellent treasure-hunting possibilities.

Abandoned Buildings

Abandoned buildings—such as an old stage stop, ranch house, or lumber camp—make good targets for coin shooters. Check out door and window frames. Scan the surface of old heavy doors. They were sometimes used for hiding coins and gold dust. Look carefully at large beams, especially on top. Valuable items are often stored on a beam and simply left there. Run your search loop the full length of all beams and over the area at the top of a door casing.

Coins found in an abandoned house.—*Photo courtesy Gene Ballinger*

From left to right, coins shown are an 1853 eagle $10 gold piece, a 1906 half-eagle $5 gold piece, and a 1909 quarter-eagle $2.50 gold piece.

Removing Dirt and Corrosion from Coins

A few coin shooting trips will probably cause several pounds of coins to accumulate in addition to the other valuables. Don't let the scruffy appearance of a long-buried coin influence an estimate of its value, and, above all, don't rush away to spend it. Not only will most such coins clean beautifully, but coin dealers and collectors will pay more than face value even for damaged specimens of certain issues because of their rarity.

Look closely with a magnifying glass at each coin uncovered, even pennies, to determine the date and mint mark. Of course, collecting this data requires removal of soil, sand,

and corrosion from the coin face. Do not, however, chemically brighten coins with commercial cleansers. Most collectors prefer the naturally aged surface of old metal, something that, once removed, cannot be restored. If a buyer desires it, he can easily change the dull surface of a coin. To enhance the chances of selling discovered coins, don't remove anything more than grime.

Plan to clean the coins from each day's search immediately after returning to the base of operations. This practice will prevent corrosion from continuing or perhaps even starting. (Coins often remain in the ground for many years without any sign of corrosion.)

To do a light cleaning job, use a soft toothbrush, warm water, and ordinary dishwashing detergent. These items, plus some delicate scrubbing, will loosen the most stubborn soil and corrosion. Add detergent at the rate of one tablespoon per pint of water. This solution will remove soil from corroded and noncorroded coins, but don't leave coins unattended, for dissimilar metal alloys may cause a damaging electrolytic action to occur.

Soak each batch in a *plastic* bowl. Do not use a *metal* container at any time or the electrolytic cell created by the dissimilar metals may destroy the coins entirely.

To clean badly corroded singles, soak them one at a time in undiluted detergent. Use a plastic cup to hold the detergent. Stay away from metal cups and check frequently on the detergent action even in the plastic cup. Brush each coin carefully.

After cleaning, rinse all coins in clean water and then isopropyl alcohol. When dry, they are ready for checking and grading.

Although this method will remove heavy corrosion, there is no way to restore metal lost to the corrosion process. These coins will always show some defacement, but if the date is one much in demand, you can sell it to a collector for use as a filler.

Coin Grades

Collectors may wish to place found coins in their own collection. Noncollectors should learn the system used to separate all coins into value groups. A coin's condition, date, and mint mark determines its numismatic value, no matter how slight or how great. The grading formulas are as follows:

About Good or *Fair* (AG-F): A badly worn coin; parts of design missing; date legible though almost worn off.

Good (G): A worn coin; all details smooth but unmistakable.

Very Good (VG): Lots of wear; some detail points not worn smooth; a little better coin than Good.

Fine (F): Wear on all high points; all features clear; design and lettering clean.

Very Fine (VF): Noticeable wear; portions of original new luster visible; details crisp.

Extremely Fine (XF): Only slight evidence of wear; more luster than VF; only highest points of detailing show wear.

About Uncirculated: Coins which have not known circulation, but which have been mishandled or jostled in the bag; coins have a fresh-from-the-mint luster, but may have some scratches.

Uncirculated: New coins intended for circulation which may have a tarnish from longtime storage; may have slight scratching; coins close to being without flaw.

Proof: Special-issue coins sold by a mint to collectors; have a flawless mirror surface.

Mint Marks

Mint marks are usually placed away from easy notice on the reverse or back sides. They are as follows:

P   Philadelphia, Pennsylvania
    (not used except on 1942-43 war nickels)

- S San Francisco, California
- D Denver, Colorado
- D Dahlonega, Georgia (gold only)
- C Charlotte, North Carolina (gold only)
- CC Carson City, Nevada
- O New Orleans, Louisiana

Determining Coin Values

The Control Coin Ready Reference Chart provides the reader with rapid access to date and mint mark combinations which, because of rarity, prove to be the ones most difficult to include in a U.S. coin collection. They are termed control or key coins. Because values change rapidly and can even vary between sections of the country, no prices are given. Naturally, the grade into which it falls partly determines the value of a coin.

In the Ready Reference Chart, the year 1909 represents a practical starting point. The main column headings indicate coin date and face value. Under the date heading the word "mint" appears; this heads the horizontal row where the letters P, D, and S occur beneath each face value indicator. These letters correspond with those occurring on the coins and stand for the name of the mint which stamped the coin (P: Philadelphia, D: Denver, S: San Francisco). These three mints are not represented in all denominations and mint years. A shaded square means no mintage for the year and government mint heading the row and column the square is in.

Because of the extraspecial value which collectors place on the 1909 VDB San Francisco mint penny, it is listed separately. (Designer Victor D. Brenner's initials appear on only 484,000 pennies stamped in 1909 at the San Francisco

DATE	CENT P	CENT D	CENT S	NICKEL P	NICKEL D	NICKEL S	DIME P	DIME D	DIME S	QUARTER P	QUARTER D	QUARTER S	HALF P	HALF D	HALF S
1909		///	C	S	///			S	S/O			S/O		/O	
VDB		///	C	///	///	///	///	///	///	///	///	///	///	///	///
1910		///	S		///			S	S			///		///	
1911			C		///				S						
1912			C		S	C			S						
1913			C	/	S/S	S/S			C						
1914		C	C		S	S			S						
1915			C			S			C						
1916							/	C	/			///	C		
1917						S								C	C
1918					/s	S						///			
1919								C	C						
1920															
1921		///	C			S	C	C				///	C	C	C
1922	C	C	///	///	///	///	///	///	///	///	///	///	///	///	///
1923		///	C		///	S	///				///		///	///	
1924		C	C		S	S							///	///	///
1925					S	S		C	C				///	///	///
1926			C			C			C				///	///	///
1927			S		S	S	C						///	///	///
1928			S		S	S							///	///	///
1929													///	///	///
1930					///	S			C		///		///	///	///
1931	S	C	C	///		C		C	C	///			///	///	///
1932	C	S	///	///	///	///	///	///	///		C	C	///	///	///
1933	C	C	///	///	///	///	///	///	///	///	///	///	///	///	///
1934			///		///			///			///			///	
1935															
1936											C				
1937												S			
1938		S	S		C					S	///			C	///

Control Coin Ready Reference Chart

DATE	CENT			NICKEL			DIME			QUARTER			HALF		
MINT	P	D	S	P	D	S	P	D	S	P	D	S	P	D	S
1939		C			C	C									
1940											S				
1941															
1942			/		C		/								
1943															
1944															
1945															
1946												S			
1947									C			S			/
1948															/
1949						C			C				S		S
1950					C	/			C						
1951						C			C						
1952									C						
1953													S		
1954									C						
1955			C			/	C	C	C		S	/	S	/	/
1956			/			/			/			/		/	/
1957			/			/			/			/		/	/
1958			/			/			/			/		/	/
1959			/			/			/			/		/	/
1960			/			/			/			/		/	/
1961			/			/			/			/		/	/
1962			/			/			/			/		/	/
1963			/			/			/			/		/	/
1964			/			/			/			/		/	/
1965			/			/			/			/		/	/
1966			/			/			/			/		/	/
1967			/			/			/			/		/	/
1968			/			/			/			/		/	/
1969			/			/			/			/		/	/

Control Coin Ready Reference Chart (*cont.*)

mint as compared to over 27,000,000 from the Philadelphia.) In all other instances where one mint issued two coin varieties in one year, a single diagonal slash divides the chart box.

The chart reveals four important facts:

1. An open box means that coins were issued in that mint, year, and denomination, but no special demand has since developed to raise prices or develop scarcity.

2. A box showing several diagonal slashes means no mintage for that mint, year, and denomination.

3. A letter "C" indicates that coins in that mint, year, and denomination are control coins. They are "keys" to a complete collection.

4. A letter "S" (two in some years and replaced by an "O" in the 1909 series to include the valuable New Orleans issues of this year) indicates that coins minted in that year, mint, and denomination are semicontrol, or are close to being key coins.

Coins Sought by Collectors

Anyone using a metal locator can make some truly valuable recoveries. The 1950D nickel, for instance, in Grade Fine will bring $10. Grade Fine special silver nickels from the years 1942 through 1945 are worth five to twenty times their face depending on year and mint mark. Lucky finders can sell even damaged ones for greater than face value because of their 35 percent silver content. The nickels in this series are easy to identify. Look for the mint mark—either a large P, D, or S—placed right over the dome of Monticello. You can't miss it. Save every five-cent piece that shows up with one of these mint marks.

Buffalo nickels, too, turn up around the places suggested in this chapter. These coins were minted from 1913 to 1938; look for the issues of 1913S, 1914D, 1921S, 1925D, 1926S, and 1931S. Collectors pay premium prices for buffalo nickels with these dates, but if you can see the date clearly on any buffalo nickel, it is worth a minimum of five times its face value. Don't sell a coin for less than it is worth on the open market.

Collectors also pay fancy prices for standing Liberty quarters. A standing Liberty quarter with the date almost gone will sell for as much as two dollars as an album filler. These coins, minted between 1916 and 1930, long ago vanished from circulation. A metal locator can still find them, however.

Half-dollars and silver dollars are harder to come by because they were not lost regularly or if lost were worth searching for until found. But you will find both halves and dollars just frequently enough to be reminded they are actually there.

Gold coins minted in 1933 and before are perfectly legal in a collection. Don't be frightened into the quick sale of a gold coin found in your sifter. You can keep it or sell it.

Driving a Bargain

To get the top price, offer your coin for sale to the highest bidder. Collectors and dealers customarily make purchases in this manner. It is the best way to sell any coin and offers reasonable certainty of getting the top market value. Place an ad describing your selections in the classified section of the local newspaper, or in *Coin World,* the numismatic weekly. Selling coins at the top market price can increase an enterprising treasure hunter's bank account handsomely.

The Great Silver Coin Disappearance

The disappearance of 90 percent silver coins from circulation has complicated the task of determining coin values. The last silver coins were minted in 1965 (in small quantity during the changeover to clad coins) and bore a 1964 date. As soon as there were enough clad coins in circulation to meet the public's need for change, the government began melting silver coins and at the same time forbade the private melting of coins. Nevertheless, speculators hoarded silver coins in anticipation of the lifting of this ban (which, in fact, has recently been rescinded). By 1967, silver coins had virtually disappeared from circulation.

The swift disappearance of silver money will affect coin collectors and coin collecting for many years to come. Even now, no one can build a collection from coins in circulation.

From a collector's viewpoint, the disappearance of the coins involved has made the records of the quantity minted suddenly meaningless. Now, lacking the old reliable measure of coin rarity and therefore worth, it will take several years to establish the true numismatic value of all the issues which have vanished.

Nobody knows just how many coins of any particular issue exist, nor can anyone predict right now just what values may develop in the future. A relatively new issue, such as a 1964 quarter, may prove to be more scarce than present hard-to-get key dates. In fact, new key dates may eventuate that, according to mintage figures, would never be less than commonplace.

Of course, millions of silver coins still exist and will continue to do so. Surviving silver coins, like the gold coins before them which escaped the melting pot, are merely out of circulation. They are hiding in private collections, misers' hoards, and coin dealers' vaults—and most important, in places where enterprising treasure hunters can find them.

chapter nine

Modern-day Methods Of Prospecting for the Hobbyist

A TREASURE hunter with a really keen interest in his hobby eventually runs out of targets in his own locality to explore. When this happens, he naturally wants to try the not-so-local-but-still-easy-to-get-to spots, and this chapter describes many of them. Experienced treasure hunters may also develop a desire to specialize and to seek targets which are out of the ordinary. Some suggestions for going about this follow.

How to Identify Possible Meteorites

Why not expand your treasure-hunting repertoire by prospecting for rare metals and minerals, such as those found in meteorites, precious stones, gold deposits scattered around the country, or lost Indian silver mines? Meteorites, for instance, are fascinating to study. Examine closely any rock that upsets a metal detector to see if it *could* be a meteorite.

Most mineralized rocks affect detectors, and it may not be possible to make a positive identification on the spot. You can tell for certain, however, when a rock specimen is *not* a meteorite. The five main points of identification follow:

1. The specimen will weigh more than other rocks of similar size.
2. A suspected meteorite will be solid, not open and porous.
3. A magnet will attract the specimen, although only weakly if the latter contains little iron. (Meteorites without at least a trace of iron are rare, but not unheard of. All the tests will apply to this group except the magnetic effect.)
4. The specimen will be black or brown on the outside. A fresh fall will be black, while one that has weathered for many years will be brown.
5. An *iron* meteorite will display a dense interior of silvery appearance similar to a section of freshly cut earth iron. (To inspect the interior, chip off a small piece of crust or grind it

Iron octhahedrite meteorite—*Photo courtesy Arizona State University Center for Meteorite Studies.*

This meteorite found at Mart, Texas, exhibits the Widmanstatten pattern characteristic of most iron meteorites.

Prospecting for the Hobbyist 147

Stony chondrite meteorite—*Photo courtesy Arizona State University Center for Meteorite Studies.*

This meteorite from Richardton, South Dakota has a black fusion crust and a stony interior.

away with a carborundum grinding wheel.) A *stony* meteorite will contain many silvery flecks scattered in a uniform manner.

Iron meteorites will be attracted strongly to a magnet. Stony meteorites will usually be attracted to a magnet, but more weakly.

Don't let meteorite look-alikes, such as smelter slag or pieces of manufactured iron, lead you astray. Suspect anything that is overly smooth or too round. If your rock has many crystals, it is not a meteorite.

If the rock specimen survives the preliminary tests and promises to pass a laboratory examination, package it together with a list of the five completed identification checks. Sign the checklist and send the package to:

> Dr. Carleton B. Moore, Director
> Center for Meteorite Studies
> Arizona State University
> Tempe, Arizona 85281

Be sure to include your name and return address. If the specimen is a meteorite, you will receive an offer for its purchase.

Precious and Semiprecious Stones

A treasure hunter should know about and make an effort to collect the precious and semiprecious jewel stones scattered around the world. Fortunately for prospectors in this country, the United States received a large share of these scattered deposits. A few are practical sources for obtaining collectors' samples.

Rubies and Sapphires

To find rubies and sapphires, go to Franklin, North Carolina. This little town is on U.S. 441 just south of Great Smoky Mountains National Park. A visit to Ruby City, the mineral treasure store in Franklin, will provide the latest information on prospecting for jewel stones in that area. Sometimes visitors find rubies of three or more karats. An unflawed three-karat stone will bring as much as $100 right there at Ruby City; so don't give up easily.

Diamonds

Treasure hunters who have had their fill of rubies and sapphires might think in terms of diamonds. No jewel box is complete without a few sparklers. Prospectors for the jewel of kings and queens can either sell their finds or have them set in personal jewelry, such as bracelets or rings.

Whatever your plans for precious stones may be, the diamonds are real enough at Murfreesboro, Arkansas. To get there, follow U.S. 70 west from Hot Springs and pick up Route 27 at Kirby. Travel south on 27 to Murfreesboro. The diamond mines are at the Crater of Diamonds, a short distance southwest of Murfreesboro. A two-dollar admission fee allows the visitor to poke around all day in the loose soil. The jewel stones found here are white, irregular crystals, and easy to recognize. In 1956 a woman found a fifteen-karat stone here worth $75,000.

Anybody planning to visit this and other similar mining areas should check in advance with the chamber of commerce located in the town closest to the place he wants to visit in order to make certain that his schedule matches theirs. A letter of inquiry, with a self-addressed return postcard enclosed, will speed the answer.

Thunder Eggs

After a spell of ruby, sapphire, and diamond mining, one might expect semiprecious stones to have little appeal, but this doesn't seem to be the case. Thunder eggs, opals, topaz, and agates stir up plenty of excitement.

Oregon specializes in thunder eggs. These agate-filled quartz nodules can be found in several Oregon localities, but the town of Prineville on U.S. 126 in the center of the state offers just about everything needed for a start. The local Chamber of Commerce will guide visitors to free claim sites where they can dig for thunder eggs, agates, jasper, and opal.

Gem Hunting in Idaho and Utah

Idaho invites almost unlimited prospecting for semiprecious stones. Seventy-two varieties exist in and about the old lava flows. Opals from Idaho are especially prized.

Utah gives precious and semiprecious stone hunters the red carpet treatment. The state has set aside special claim sites for visitors where anybody can dig. Send a card to the Utah Travel Council, Salt Lake City, Utah 84114. Ask for their bulletin of rock hunting instruction for visitors.

Topaz and Fairy Stones

Other areas of the country promote their own particular specialties. Texas boasts an unusual variety of topaz which can be found in Mason County. Virginians talk about the "fairy stones" which come from Fairy Stone State Park, off State Highway 57.

Agates

Lake Superior's beaches offer agate hunters a thrill. Beachcombers pick up truly beautiful specimens here daily from the moment the ice goes out until the lake freezes over once again. Public access sites abound along the southern shore of Lake Superior, but only a few people, out of the many who use them, venture beyond the area visible from the parking lots. The best hunting, logically, lies beyond these heavily used portions.

Agates are also particularly plentiful on the Pacific coast. One of the best spots in the country is Agate Beach in Patrick Point State Park near the northern border of California. In Oregon, agates can be found not only along the beaches but throughout the interior. For information, write to Oregon Department of Geology and Mineral Industries in Salem.

Rock shops constantly seek quality agate specimens, and they will usually buy all they can get.

Prospecting for Gold

Precious and semiprecious rocks and specimen crystals occur in areas which at some period of time in their geological his-

Prospecting for the Hobbyist 151

Hunting for agates on the shore of Lake Superior.

tory underwent heat, pressure, and later upheaval. Gold deposits were created in generally the same areas and during the same time periods.

Some few billion years ago, the elements which today are cool and solid were hot and gassy. Gradually these gases began to cool down. A few eons later the entire hot mud pie fell in on itself, and out of this came our present assortment of rocks, metals, and crystals. In certain places, areas of weakness developed on the earth's surface, and the cooling solids were pushed upward in great jagged masses. Some of these upheavals brought gold-bearing quartz to the surface. Today a land area where quartz imprisons gold is known as mother lode country. In northern California, where mother lode country spreads over thousands of square miles, panic-driven men in 1849 literally ran one another down to get at this gold. It was not a difficult thing to do, for the precious metal lay in bits and pieces all over the super-rich gravel washed down from the mountains.

Legend to Gold Bearing Rivers

1. Platte
2. South Platte
3. Cheyenne
4. Belle Fourche
5. Snake
6. Salmon
7. Columbia
8. Calapooya
9. Rogue
10. Klamath
11. Pit
12. Trinity
13. Feather
14. Yuba
15. Bear
16. Sacramento
17. Cosumnes
18. Mokelumne
19. Calaveras
20. Stanislaus
21. Tuolumne
22. San Joaquin
23. Merced
24. Chowchilla
25. Fresno
26. Placerita
27. San Gabriel
28. Walker
29. Carson
30. Humboldt
31. Reese
32. Colorado
33. San Juan
34. Rio Grande
35. Arkansas
36. Mulberry (Chilton)*
37. Chulafinnee Creek (Cleburne)
38. Baggs Branch (Lumpkin)
39. Etowah (Lumpkin)
40. Chestatee (Lumpkin)
41. Yahoolah Creek (Lumpkin)
42. Whitewater (Oconee)
43. Texaway (Oconee)
44. Valley (Cherokee)
45. Coker Creek (Monroe)
46. Whippoorwill (Monroe)
47. Brush Creek (Floyd)
48. Laurel Creek (Floyd)
49. Indian Creek (Coos)
50. Swift (Franklin)

---

*Where the gold-bearing characteristic is localized, the pertinent county is included.

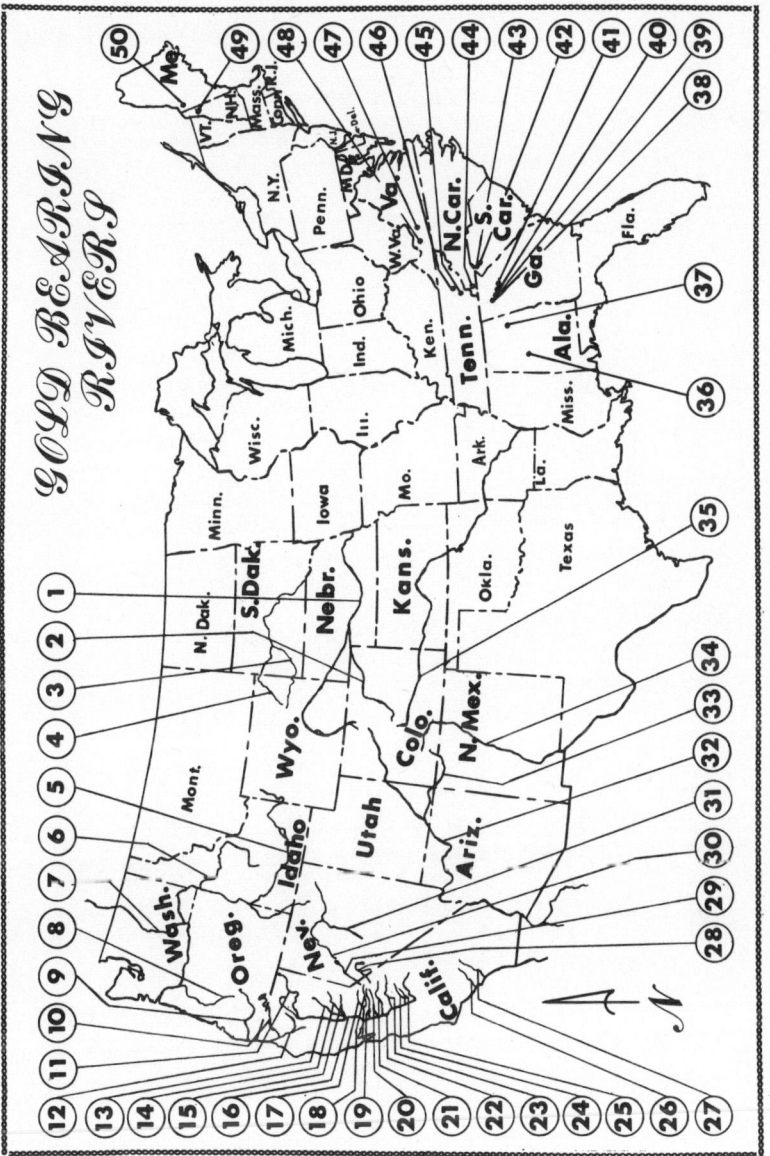

Gold-bearing Rivers and Streams

Some of this gold-laden gravel was washed into rivers. Known gold-producing streams run all over the western half of the country, but the East has some too. Following are some tips on gold-bearing streams in various states:

California: There are too many rivers to list, but count the Butte, North Fork of the Yuba, Feather, Rubicon, and American among the principal gold-bearing streams. All tributaries to these rivers must be considered part of the system.

Colorado: Try Cripple Creek, where a gold field opened in 1891; also the upper Colorado, the Arkansas, the upper Rio Grande, San Juan, South Platte, and Eagle rivers.

Georgia: Have a go at any stream along the north border.

Idaho: Check the Kootenai and the Snake River gravels. Both carry gold.

Kansas: The Arkansas River is the best bet here.

Montana: The Yaak River in Lincoln County is considered to be a gold river.

Nebraska: Try the South Platte River.

Nevada: Check the Reese and Humboldt rivers, also the Carson and Walker rivers; lots of gold sands here.

North Carolina: Try the streams which rise in Georgia.

Oregon: The Bear and Rogue rivers are the likeliest prospects.

South Dakota: Try the Fourche and Cheyenne rivers, as well as streams flowing into them.

Washington: The Columbia River gravels contain gold.

Wyoming, Montana, and South Dakota: The Yellowstone River flows through these three major gold-producing states. Check the tributaries.

The bottom gravels of Canadian streams also contain gold. It is considered to be in rich supply along the Quebec-Ontario border. Check out the St. Maurice and Nottaway Bell rivers and tributary streams. British Columbia may someday be an important gold producer; check the headwaters of the Kootenai, Thompson, Fraser, and Quesnel rivers.

Underwater Prospecting Gear

Underwater prospecting for gold was virtually unknown before the year 1950, because this type of prospecting requires special gear. By 1950, some of the then new scuba users began to think about using their equipment for underwater prospecting. It turned out to be a fabulous idea. Although professionals today do their underwater prospecting with hookah (compressor, hose, and mask) rather than scuba, scuba divers today search for gold as a vacation hobby in every accessible and not-so-accessible corner of the North and South American continents.

The forty-niners used pans, pick, shovel, and sluice box to separate heavy gold particles from the lighter gravels. Today's underwater prospector relies on a wet suit and a centrifugal or air lift floating dredge to pump river bottom sediment up to his riffle box. The air lift dredge provides an inexpensive method for working in water that is five feet or more in depth. Commercial surface dredges such as the Keene 2½-inch Model 2500 work well in water only a few inches deep, using a centrifugal pump to operate a venturi. Both types of dredges are positioned to discharge into a riffle box or sieve designed to trap heavy metal particles such as coins, rings, or nuggets.

The dredge sucks up large quantities of sediment and sorts out the gold flakes and nuggets which settle to river bottoms and lodge in cracks and crevices. You can build a small working model of an air lift dredge in a home workshop from polyvinyl chloride plastic pipe, or purchase a larger commercial aluminum unit for a few dollars more.

The accompanying diagrams illustrate a homemade air lift dredge employing polyvinyl chloride plastic pipe. To use it for river prospecting, substitute a riffle box for the wire basket.

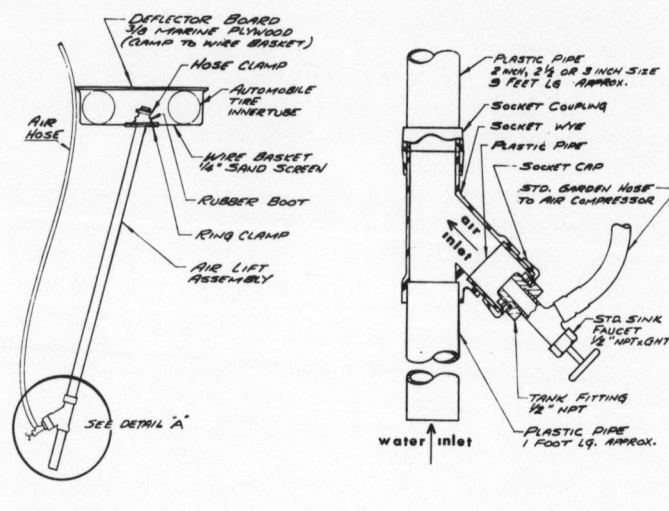

Homemade air lift dredge.   Detail A

We chose polyvinyl chloride plastic pipe for a construction material because hardware and plumbing supply stores everywhere sell it. Use either plastic pressure pipe or drain pipe. The fittings are standard and available wherever plastic plumbing supplies are sold.

A common, cord-reinforced garden hose feeds compressed air to the lower end of the pipe (air pressure should not exceed 50 pounds per square inch). A salvaged refrigerator compressor driven by a 2- or 3-horsepower gasoline engine will usually supply this small air lift up to depths of 10 feet. Details of the air inlet construction are shown by Detail A, containing the following abbreviations: STD. = standard, LG. = length, NPT = National Pipe Thread, and GHT = Garden Hose Thread.

Prospecting for the Hobbyist

The air lift assembly shown in the diagrams is basic to all air lift design. Actual construction may vary to suit the end use and material available. Modifications usually center around increasing the air flow volume at the nozzle and extending the length of the hose above water to allow the outflow to take place away from the dredging site.

Operation is as follows: The compressor injects compressed air at any pressure above the surrounding water pressure at the nozzle site a short distance above the nozzle opening. The air immediately expands and begins to ascend the tube. As the air expands, its pressure decreases quickly to a level well below the surrounding water pressure. Water, being noncompressible, cannot expand to equalize the lowered pressure at the open nozzle end. Theoretically, an entire river or lake will try to enter the open nozzle end in order to equalize the pressure loss caused by the rising, expanding air column. In practical terms what actually happens is that a strong current of water spurts up the pipe. The current appears as suction at the nozzle opening, and any ob-

Air lift dredge used to remove sand from wreck site in the Caribbean.—*Photo courtesy Calvin Deviney*

ject that will flow through the tube will be carried to the surface and expelled with considerable force into the receiver. Coins, rings, stones, keys, nuggets, sand, and mud all go flying up the tube. The riffle box keeps the flying objects from getting back in the water.

Underwater prospecting equipment must be portable. A typical team of two will pack everything on their backs needed for a one-week prospecting trip. It will consist of food, hoses, sluice box, air compressor, two-cycle gasoline engine, two five-gallon gas cans, centrifugal pump, and a couple of truck tire inner tubes for flotation.

Underwater prospecting is not for people who dislike rough living, cold water, and hard work. But an adventurous person can expect to at least make expenses from underwater prospecting and at the same time enjoy life to the absolute limit. Fortunately, the rivers work constantly for you by washing golden flakes, fines, and nuggets from their quartz prison to position them for the dredge tube.

Gold Panning

The use of a portable dredge to vacuum clean the bottom of a mother lode river represents the most advanced state of the art. Gold hunters, however, can get by without a dredge by making use of the time-tried method which employs a gold pan.

Nuggets, dust, and flakes still abound throughout the California fields, but panning, to be worthwhile, must be applied to rich gold-bearing gravels and sands. Such material is difficult to locate in the western mother lode states. This is not entirely so in the case of the Georgia gold-bearing areas. In fact, the gold-bearing creeks and rivers of northern Georgia may yield big profits to gold divers who know how to use an air lift dredge.

Gold mining activity in Georgia centers around a little town called Dahlonega. It is located in the northern part of the state approximately fifty air miles north of Atlanta. To get there by car from Atlanta, simply follow U.S. 19 north. Going by car, you must travel a few miles more, but the scenery is terrific.

Dahlonega, which in Cherokee refers to the yellow metal once abundant in the area, experienced America's first gold rush. The U.S. government even set a mint up here to make use of the gold supply, and there is still plenty of gold left in the hills and streams of northern Georgia. Streams and creeks tributary to the Chestatee River, or those rising north of Dahlonega in the hills of Crown Mountain, could provide a careful worker with some of the best gold panning yet remaining in the United States.

To have a go at gold panning without the need to purchase equipment and at a site where instruction is available, stop at the gold museum at Dahlonega. Here you can borrow a gold pan and get instruction in its proper use. A short distance from the museum you can scoop pay dirt into the pan and wash it down to the gold fines with water from a mountain pond. You won't find so many large nuggets as small flakes, but it *is* genuine gold.

A word of caution: prospecting for gold is not recommended as a way of making a living. You may get rich from a lucky strike, but such good fortune is rare. The average hard-working diver will make $10 one day and maybe $30 on the next. On an especially good day the take may go to $50. Only a few lucky prospectors get back more than expenses. Many more fail to get even this much. Prospecting for gold should be a vacation or spare-time activity. Smart prospectors who follow the rivers will at least never suffer from thirst.

Avoid hard-rock prospecting for gold. It wastes too much time to be considered as a hobby activity and, considering its danger and difficulty, is not even much of a full-time occupation.

Steps in Gold Panning

1. Using a clean, rust-free pan with smooth, dentless bottom and sides, fill pan slightly less than three-quarters full. 2. Totally immerse pan and contents in water (flowing water will maintain clarity). With the pan underwater, reduce the bulk by breaking up the larger chunks of clay or dirt and allowing the water to carry away the pieces, and by removing large stones and rock fragments. 3. Move the pan in a circle to create a current, occasionally bringing the swirling motion to an abrupt halt. This will stratify the sediments so that those of light specific gravity will occupy the top layer (where you can wash them away) while materials of high specific gravity (including gold) will migrate to the bottom. 4. When nothing remains in the pan but heavy black sand and gold, known as "concentrates," extract the gold flakes with tweezers or amalgamate them later with mercury.

Lost Indian Silver Mines

Treasure seekers who get tired of prospecting for gold can try their hand at exploring for silver. In Ohio, the lure of lost silver mines continues as strong as it was 150 years ago. The Indians who once inhabited the lands now called Ohio were mining silver somewhere in the state, but they took great care to preserve the secret of the location. Few clues remain which could help to solve the mystery. There are, however, some legends. One persistent legend concerns silver mines located on Massies Creek in Green County, close to the site of present-day Wilberforce University.

Michigan is also host to a lost Indian silver mine legend. From the sketchy evidence available, Indian tribes once worked a mine which occupied the area known today as the Copper Country. This region contains silver, and the abundant native copper mined here is often alloyed with silver. The Indian miners, however, according to stories brought back by early explorers, were getting pure silver. But when the Indians were forced to leave, they took the secret of their silver mine with them.

The best place to begin a search for this lost Michigan mine would be the Porcupine Mountains. This huge tract of state-owned land is located on the south shores of Lake Superior, twenty-five miles west of Ontonagan. The fine state park here makes a good base of operations. You can camp for two weeks in one place for a small daily fee. In fact, for a campground located far from civilization, this one is as complete as can be found anywhere. And, to provide a change from climbing up and down hills on a search for lost silver mines, almost endless agate beaches, mentioned earlier in this chapter, stretch east and west from the campground.

No matter which treasure one chooses to hunt—meteorites, precious stones, gold, or silver—the earth jealously guards vast riches which she will surrender only to those who have the equipment, skill, and patience to uncover them.

chapter ten

Obligations of the Treasure Hunter

TREASURE hunting pays rich dividends in fun, profit, and adventure, but entails many obligations—to the owners of lost items and properties searched, to the government, to the general public, and to other treasure hunters.

Respecting Private Property

Diligent research may point to the existence of treasure on private property, but this presents certain problems. The owner may challenge a treasure hunter's presence on his property. The only way to guard against this is to get permission before entering private property, an easy task if the request is made properly. Approach a property owner or caretaker with a businesslike and friendly manner. Come right out with your purpose. Don't hide behind half-truths. Offer to share one-half the value, if necessary, of whatever items are found.

Search and Salvage Agreements

If private property hides what you believe to be an especially valuable treasure hoard, make certain that permission to explore the property is in writing, with agreement for division of the trove. Fifty-fifty is not unreasonable.

Now suppose a map leads to a fenced-off 100-year-old empty house. Keep out until the owner can be located. Don't reveal any more than necessary of your conclusions about the old house, but do try for permission to make an electronic search of all parts of the premises. Again, an agreement in writing will tend to make believers out of uncooperative people.

Returning Property to Owners

It doesn't take long for a skillful treasure hunter to accumulate enough odds and ends to start a secondhand ring and rusty watch shop. Some of the rings may be of extraordinary value with an even chance of finding the owners. Most of the money found will be absolutely beyond claim by anybody except the person who got there first. But occasionally cash finds may have identifying marks. In such a case, make every attempt to return the find to its owner. For instance, if you happen to recover a money bag full of cash, and the bag is marked "Homesteaders' Savings and Loan Association," the bag's contents probably belong to the savings association. If such is the case, they will be overjoyed to get it back and you may get a cash reward.

Of course, it doesn't hurt, on the occasion of finding a full money bag, to inquire about rewards *before* turning the cash over to the authorities. But each of us has his own way of handling such problems. It is really a personal matter. The important thing to remember is that an effort should always be made to return recovered valuables to rightful owners.

Here are some examples of what happened when large sums of money were found. Roger Ashy, Ardie McDonald,

SEARCH AND SALVAGE AGREEMENT

This agreement, dated this _____ day of _____, 19 _____, between _____ and _____ his wife, hereinafter known as the Property Owners, and_____, hereinafter known as the Salvagor,

WITNESSES:

In consideration of the Salvagor's undertaking to devote his time and equipment in a search of the premises described as: *

_____

_____

_____

the Property Owners hereby agree that the Salvagor shall receive as compensation for his services

_____ of all money, jewelry, artifacts, and _____
(one half or other fraction)

_____, which may have been lost or concealed in, on, or about the above premises and discovered by the Salvagor.

The Salvagor is given full authority to work in, on, or about the said premises at any reasonable time, subject only to such notice as the Property Owners may require in advance of such work. Each party waives any possible claim against the other for liability for any careless or negligent act or omission of the other arising out of or in consequence of the search herein provided for.

This agreement shall be effective for _____ months from the date hereof.

Executed at _____, _____.

_____   _____
Salvagor   Property Owner

                                                                _____
                                                                Property Owner

* NOTE: Property may be described generally as a house and lot, or a farm or tract of a particular street or road address, owned by the Property Owners, or by use of the legal description, if available.

and Jerry Self of Centralia, Illinois found $11,200 in a glass jar on an unoccupied farm. They turned the money over to the police. The police found the owner.

Clifford O'Rourke and Scott Leas of St. Paul, Minnesota found close to $3000 in St. Paul's Cherokee Park. They turned the package over to the police. In this case, the owner could not be located and Scott and Cliff got the money.

Julie Doyle of Hull, Massachusetts found a silver coin on a local beach and started a big treasure hunt. People flocked in from everywhere. Many more coins were recovered, but the main cache probably remains undiscovered. These coins could not be identified as belonging to anybody. Finders keepers.

At Grand Rapids, Michigan, two grade-school boys found $50,000 in an old table under several layers of moldering cardboard. The boys were not convinced that the bills were real, but their parents were more objective. The family turned the money over to the Grand Rapids police department. After six weeks of intensive effort, the police located the rightful owner of the errant cash, an elderly woman who had hidden the money in the table for safekeeping.

At Chamblee, Georgia, Larry Ledbetter found $19,635.51 in an old suitcase covered by leaves. It was identified as loot from a bank robbery and returned to the owners.

At Lake City, Minnesota a St. Paul man dug up two mason jars full of silver dollars and half-dollars in an area used as a bootlegger hangout during the days of the Volstead Act. The owner of this money cache would be impossible to locate. In such cases the loot can be kept by the finder.

How to Avoid Litigation

Unless an owner of lost money or merchandise publicly gives up his title to it, it remains the legal property of the owner at the time of loss. Some treasure hunters, however, sincerely believe that when the *official* search for missing property is abandoned, regardless of how it was lost in the first place, then so is the title. Then, too, there are individuals who care nothing for the fact that they have no legal claim to a particular treasure found by somebody else. This type will go after it anyway.

For all the above reasons, disputes about found treasure sometimes land in court. When this happens, it is usually a sad day for everybody concerned. Treasure hunters who keep this in mind will not find it hard to choose between adding to their bank account and front-page newspaper publicity.

The Income Tax

The Internal Revenue Service is not in business to tell citizens what they may or may not do to earn money. But they insist on the government's due when it is time to collect the tax owed on that money you earned—or dug up.

Treasure hunters who earn substantial sums from their hobby should seek the advice of a tax consultant. Agents of the IRS, of course, will also furnish information on reporting income from treasure-hunting activities. Every large city has numbers of these revenue men. Look them up in the phone book.

Ordinarily, you will not be challenged if you report treasure trove on the tax form as miscellaneous income, but this classification does not provide any way to deduct expenses. Most treasure hunters treat money earned from their hobby as self-employment income and file schedule C with their returns. Whatever you do, be sure to report all your treasure-hunting income.

Avoiding the Stigma of Vandalism

A professional treasure hunter always cleans up after himself.

There is, however, a perverse type who loves to dig, but not fill, gaping holes in sod; even beautiful park lawns get no mercy from this fellow. He delights in tearing treadboards from stairways, trim boards from door casings, and paneling from walls—none of it ever to be replaced. Stay away from places that have received this treatment. You could be blamed for the mess.

Repairing Sod

Do not leave unfilled holes behind you, especially those made in sod. You can remove coins from any lawn without visible damage to the grass. It takes only a little practice to learn the correct way to use a detector and how to retrieve the target.

Try first on some unimportant grass on your own lawn. Move the loop across the target area until an exact bearing is obtained on the buried item. Now select the slender ten-inch screwdriver from your kit and use it to carefully probe the target area for a strike on something solid. This slim-bodied tool slips easily into the sod bed, and by skillful probing it will determine whether the site contains a coin, a bottle cap, or a ring. The screwdriver also provides an accurate measure of target depth.

A coin buried less than two inches deep can be pried out with a heavier screwdriver. If the target lies five or six inches below the surface, it is necessary to remove a small plug of grass. Do this carefully with a *sharp*-edged garden trowel. Extract the coin or whatever and replace the soil and sod plug. Press a heel into the filled area until the spot is level with the surroundings.

Some thoughtful types sprinkle a few grass seeds on a repaired area. If you do strew a few grass seeds around, use only annual rye. Adding grass seed to a plug is not really necessary, but these holes must be well filled and the grass replaced.

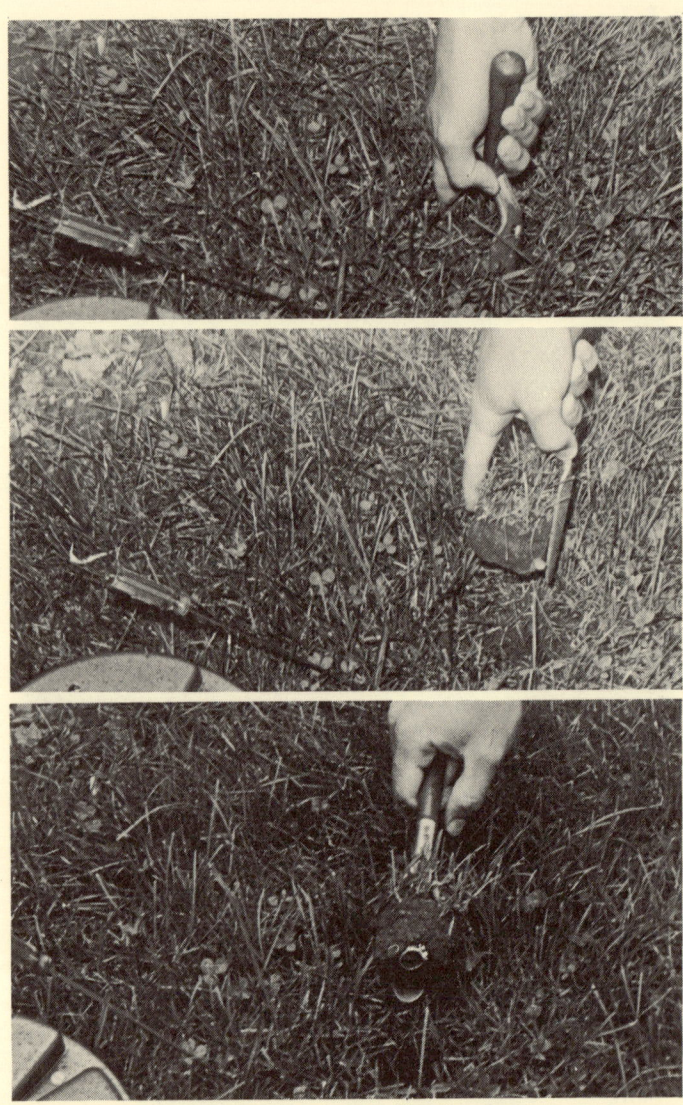

Steps in Lifting a Grass Plug from Sod

Top: Cut a 2- to 3-inch diameter circle with the garden trowel. *Center:* Hold a firm pressure with the trowel and lift the plug from the hole. *Bottom:* Extract the target metal and replace the plug.

Replacing Trim Boards

Unfortunately, the same individuals who leave holes unfilled are also destructive in other places. They leave calling cards of broken plaster, loose planks, ripped-up stair steps and flooring, and so on.

It's easy to tell when damage in an abandoned building is the work of a treasure hunter. Abused doorways are the clue. A careless hunter will fail to replace trim boards pried from door frame lintels. These spots are standard hiding places and should always be searched when exploring an abandoned building. But replace the trim board.

Tipping Off Treasure Hunters Who Follow You

Before you replace a lintel close-out board, put a couple of tin cans or a few pieces of aluminum foil inside the opening. Such a deposit will tell the next treasure hunter on the scene that the building has been searched. This practice prevails among people in the know.

Use the same friendly tipoff anywhere an excavation is required to get at a treasure hoard. If *you* find cans or trash at the bottom of a hole, congratulations on being in line behind another treasure hunter with class. The other fellow probably got the treasure you were looking for. But the thing to be thankful for, when encountering this situation, is being notified of the fact that the treasure is gone. This type of message prevents treasure hunters who arrive late from wasting more time. Of course, it's crushing to learn that somebody else got there first, but knowing it can save hours, even days, of fruitless searching.

Be encouraged. You'll probably be first at the site of the next cache.

Metal Detector Manufacturers

Heath Company
Benton Harbor, Mich. 49022

White's Electronics, Inc.
1011 Pleasant Valley Rd.
Sweet Home, Oreg. 97386

Garrett Electronics
P.O. Box 28434
Dallas, Tex. 75228

Metrotech Underground Explorations
Box 793
Menlo Park, Calif. 94025

Gardiner Electronics Co.
4729 N. 7th Ave.
Phoenix, Ariz. 85013

Fisher Research Laboratory
1890 Embarcadero Rd.
Palo Alto, Calif. 94303

Detectron
P.O. Box 281
San Gabriel, Calif. 91778

D-Tex Electronics
P.O. Box 246
Garland, Tex. 75041

The Goldak Co., Inc.
1101-A Air Way
Glendale, Calif. 91201

Rayscope Co.
P.O. Box 715
North Hollywood, Calif. 91603

Electronic Parts Supply Houses

Allied Radio Shack
100 N. Western Ave.
Chicago, Ill. 60680
 (Catalog available on request)

Lafayette Radio Electronics
111 Jerico Turnpike
Syosset, L.I., N.Y. 11791
 (Catalog available on request)

Olson Electronics
260 S. Forge St.
Akron, Ohio 44308
 (Catalog available on request)

Burstein-Applebee
3199 Mercier St.
Kansas City, Mo. 64111
 (Catalog available on request)

McGee Radio Co.
1901-07 McGee St.
Kansas City, Mo. 64108
 (Catalog available on request)

Publishers of Treasure-Hunting Periodicals

The Association
P.O. Box 412
Oscoda, Mich. 48750

The Gold Bug
P.O. Box 588
Alamo, Calif. 94507

National Prospectors Gazette
Segundo, Colo. 81070

National Treasure Hunters League
Box 53
Mesquite, Tex. 75149

Northwest Treasure News
Box 5075
Spokane, Wash. 99205

Prospectors Club International
P.O. Box 548
Midland, Tex. 79701

The Treasure Hunter
P.O. Box 188
Midway City, Calif. 92655

Treasure News
P.O. Box 614
Torrance, Calif. 90508

True Treasure (and Treasure World)
P.O. Drawer L
Conroe, Tex. 77301

Western Treasures
P.O. Box 845
Reseda, Calif. 91335

Recommended Reading

Books

Albano, Charles M. *Beachcombing for Treasure or Pleasure.* Alamo, Calif.: Gold Bug, 1969.

Allen, Gina. *Gold!* New York: Thomas Y. Crowell Co., 1964.

Beard, Charles R. *The Romance of Treasure Trove.* London: S. Low, Marston & Co., 1933.

Bell, Robert. *A Treasure Guide.* La Crosse, Wisc.: Specialty Products, 1968.

Blanchard, Fessenden S. *Ghost Towns of New England.* New York: Dodd, Mead & Co., 1960.

Bowen, Dana T. *Shipwrecks of the Lakes.* Daytona Beach: Privately printed, 1952.

Bradley, Van Allen. *Gold in Your Attic.* New York: Fleet Publishing Corp., 1958.

Burney, James. *History of the Buccaneers of America.* 1816. Reprint. New York: Barnes & Noble, 1951.

Carnahan, J. W. *4000 Civil War Battles.* 1899. Reprint. Toyahvale, Tex.: Frontier Book Co., 1962.

Carse, Robert. *The Age of Piracy*. New York: Rinehart & Co., 1957.

Caruso, John A. *The Great Lakes Frontier*. Indianapolis: Bobbs-Merrill Co., 1961.

Chambers, Howard V. *Dowsers, Divining Rods and Water Witches for the Millions*. Los Angeles: Sherbourne Press, 1969.

Chastain, Dayne. *101 Easy Ways to Find Buried Treasure*. Seminole, Okla.: Privately printed, 1965.

Chidsey, Donald B. *The American Privateers*. New York: Dodd, Mead & Co., 1962.

Cooke, Nelson M., ed. *Electronics Data Handbook*. Chicago: Allied Radio Corp., 1963.

Cooper, Gordon. *Treasure-Trove, Pirates' Gold*. New York: Wilfred Funk, 1951.

Dow, George F., and Edmonds, John H. *Pirates of the New England Coast*. Salem, Mass.: The Marine Research Society, 1923.

Exquemelin, Alexandre Olivier [Esquemeling, John], *The Buccaneers of America*. 1678. Reprint. London: George Allen & Unwin, 1951.

Ferguson, Robert G. *Lost Treasure: The Search for Hidden Gold*. New York: Vantage Press, 1957.

Ferris, Robert G., ed. *Explorers and Settlers*. Washington, D.C.: National Park Service, 1968.

Florin, Lambert. *Western Ghost Towns*. Seattle: Superior Publishing Co., 1961.

Fredericks, Dean. *John Dillinger*. New York: Pyramid Books, 1962.

Gibson, Walter B., and Litzka, R. *The Illustrated Book of the Psychic Sciences*. New York: Doubleday & Co., 1966.

Gladson, Deek. *Sudden Wealth*. Alamo, Calif.: Gold Bug, 1964.

Glasscock, C. B. *Gold in Them Hills*. Indianapolis: Bobbs-Merrill Co., 1932.

Gosse, Philip. *The History of Piracy*. New York: Tudor Publishing Co., 1934.

Griffith, S. V. *Alluvial Prospecting and Mining*. New York: Pergamon Press, 1960.

Havinghurst, Walter. *Wilderness for Sale*. American Procession Series. New York: Hastings House Publishers, 1956.

Hogg, Gary. *Lust for Gold*. New York: A. S. Barnes and Co., 1960.

Homsher, Lola M., ed. *South Pass, 1868—James Chisholm's Journal of the Wyoming Gold Rush*. Lincoln: University of Nebraska Press, 1960.

Horner, Dave. *Shipwrecks, Skin Divers, and Sunken Gold*. New York: Dodd, Mead & Co., 1965.

Hungerford, Edward. *Wells Fargo—Advancing the American Frontier*. New York: Random House, 1949.

Johnson, Charles. *A History of the Robberies and Murders of the Most Notorious Highwaymen and Pyrates*. London: J. Janeway, 1734.

Jones, Katherine M. *When Sherman Came*. New York: Bobbs-Merrill Co., 1964.

Kendall, Charles W. *Private Men of War*. London: P. Allan and Co., 1931.

Lyle, John H. *The Dry and Lawless Years*. New York: Prentice-Hall, 1960.

Malkus, Alida. *Blue-Water Boundary*. New York: Hastings House Publishers, 1960.

Masefield, John. *On the Spanish Main*. New York: The Macmillan Co., 1925.

Morgan, Bev. *Diving with Safety*. Los Angeles: U.S. Divers Co., 1956.

Mueller, Karl von. *Encyclopedia of Buried Treasure Hunting*. Weeping Water, Nebr.: Examino Press, 1965.

Paine, Ralph D. *The Book of Buried Treasure*. New York: The Macmillan Co., 1911.

Potter, John S., Jr. *The Treasure Diver's Guide*. New York: Doubleday & Co., 1960.

Pringle, Patrick. *Jolly Roger*. New York: W. W. Norton & Co., 1953.

Prucha, Francis P. *Guide to Military Posts of the United States*. Harrisburg, Pa.: The Stackpole Co., 1966.

Ransom, Jay Ellis. *A Range Guide to Mines and Minerals*. New York: Harper & Row, 1964.

Rascoe, Jesse E. *The Golden Crescent*. Toyahvale, Tex.: Frontier Book Co., 1962.

Renne, Harold S. *Electronic Metal Locators*. Indianapolis: Howard W. Sams & Co., 1956.

Roosevelt, Theodore. *The Naval War of 1812*. New York: Charles Scribner's Sons, 1926.

Smith, Warren. *Finders Keepers*. New York: Belmont Publications, 1967.

Steiger, Brad. *Treasure Hunting*. New York: Ace Books, 1967.

Sternbeck, Alfred. *Filibusters and Buccaneers*. New York: Robert M. McBride and Co., 1930.

Traywick, Ben. *Treasures of the Dead*. Tombstone, Ariz.: *The Tombstone Epitaph*, 1967.

Verril, Hyatt A. *In the Wake of the Buccaneers*. New York: The Century Co., 1923.

Webb, Todd. *Gold Strikes and Ghost Towns*. New York: Doubleday & Co., 1961.

Whipple, A. B. C. *The Pirate Rascals of the Spanish Main*. New York: Doubleday & Co., 1957.

Willoughby, Malcolm F. *Rum War at Sea*. Washington, D.C.: U.S. Government Printing Office, 1964.

Wycherly, George. *Buccaneers of the Pacific*. Indianapolis: Bobbs-Merrill Co., 1928.

Magazine Articles

Anderson, Dick. "$500 Weekend." *Skin Diver*, July 1968, pp. 28-31.

———. "Gold Comes in Quartz." *Skin Diver*, October 1963, pp. 20-28.

———. "There Is Gold on the Winfield Scott." *Skin Diver*, September 1969, pp. 28-31.

Arnett, Judd. "Heavens—Remember the Volstead Act?" *Detroit Free Press*, 29 October 1969, p. 10D.

Atwater, James. "Spanish Gold Two Fathoms Deep." *Saturday Evening Post*, 12 December 1964, pp. 66-71.

Bruce, Max H. "Crossroads of the Pioneers." *Our Public Lands*, Summer 1970, pp. 11-14.

Recommended Reading

Buchanan, T. G. "Largest Underwater Treasure Hunt." *Sea Frontiers,* January 1969, pp. 21-29.

Cahill, Robert E. "New England Treasure Wrecks." *Skin Diver,* December 1964, pp. 52-57.

Clark, Allan B. "We Found the Lost Millions of Manila Bay." *Saturday Evening Post,* 13 September 1952, pp. 19-21.

Clarke, Jafar. "Who Gets to Keep the Goodies?" *True Treasure,* Fall 1966, pp. 18-25.

"Combing New Jersey's Beaches." *Gold Bug Annual No. 1,* 1964, p. 3.

Day, Joe. "Discover the Apostles." *Lakeland Boating,* May 1969, pp. 22-26.

De Camp, Michael. "Wreck of the San Diego." *Skin Diver,* April 1966, p. 29.

Deviney, Calvin A. "Air Lifts." *Compressed Air Magazine,* April 1967, pp. 13-16.

Fitzgerald, Floyd. "More About Beachcombing." *Treasure Hunter* 2, no. 6, pp. 5-7.

Fulks, Patricia D. "Hunting Civil War Relics." *True Treasure,* April 1970, pp. 29-32.

Goodman, Martin. "New Silver Coin Boom." *Coin Mart,* Fall 1969, pp. 23-24.

Green, Vaughn M. "Oak Island." *Treasure Annual No. 7,* pp. 32-34.

Hartley, William and Ellen. "Anyone for Millions." *Pageant,* July 1966, pp. 60-67.

Hollister, Frederick F. "How to Market Your Treasure Finds." *True Treasure,* December 1969, pp. 21-23.

Horner, Dave. "The Golden Galleons." *Skin Diver,* April 1965, pp. 28-32.

Iams, J. "Anyone for Buried Treasure." *Saturday Evening Post,* 13 June 1964, pp. 64-66.

"In Search of the Lost Dutchman Mine." *Friends,* November 1969, pp. 2-5.

Janowski, Alan. "Coin Beach." *True Treasure,* Fall 1967, p. 63.

Kiedrowski, Leonard. "Treasure of the Apostles." *Treasure World,* February-March 1970, pp. 25-26.

King, Fred L. "Did Dillinger Bury $200,000 at Little Bohemia?" *True Treasure,* Winter 1966, pp. 52-56.

Lasco, Jack. "Captain Kidd's Lost $21 Million." *Saga,* May 1966, pp. 9-11.

Mahan, William. "I Find Little Treasures." *Frontier Times,* August-September 1963, pp. 32-33 and October-November 1963, pp. 44-45.

Manieri, Raymond. "Royal Fifth." *Skin Diver,* April 1967, pp. 26-29.

Martin, Lee. "New Crisis in Silver." *Coin Age,* August 1967, pp. 18-19.

Marx, Bob. "Secrets of a Professional Treasure Diver." *Argosy,* August 1968, pp. 50-53.

"Million Dollar Spanish Treasure." *Skin Diver,* February 1967, p. 27.

"New Group to Back Oak Island Treasure Hunt." *Coin World,* 17 December 1969, p. 54.

Onellion, James. "The Fortunes and Misfortunes of Gold Diving." *Skin Diver,* July 1964, pp. 22-25.

"On the Tail of Treasure." *Allstate Motor Club Magazine,* Autumn 1969, pp. 16-19.

Paterson, T. W. "Treasure of the Brother Jonathan." *Treasure World,* November 1969, pp. 24-27.

Phibbs, Corbett. "Miniball Bonanza." *Skin Diver,* August 1970, pp. 16-19.

Quebedeaux, Earl. "1764 Tragedy Here Recalled." *Cleveland Plain Dealer,* 30 June 1968.

"Red Taped Gold." *Life,* 21 July 1952, pp. 37-40.

"Silver Melt Could Make New Keys." *Coin World,* 17 December 1969, p. 8.

Simonsen, Svend T. "Your Best Friend—The Compass." *Yachting,* June 1970, p. 72.

Stackpole, Peter. "Wreck Hunting with the Master." *Skin Diver,* February 1969, pp. 45-47.

Stenuit, R. "Priceless Relics of the Spanish Armada." *National Geographic,* June 1969, pp. 745-777.

Strong, C. L. "Building a Magnetometer." *Scientific American,* February 1968, pp. 124-128.

Tzimoulis, Paul J. "Connecticut Wreck and Sunken Treasure." *Skin Diver,* November 1965, pp. 14-21.

Recommended Reading

Wharton, Don. "Those Florida Treasure Hunts." *Reader's Digest,* June 1968, pp. 202-204.

"Who Gets the Gold." *Newsweek,* 18 April 1964, p. 64.

Wilber, Robert. "Pick and Spade Fishing." *Our Public Lands,* Fall 1968, pp. 8-10.

Willis, Ivan B. "The Secret of Fifty Mile Mountain." *Our Public Lands,* Fall 1968, pp. 16-17.

Winters, Frank. "John Dillinger's Missing $1 Million Dollar Bank Loot." *Argosy,* July 1968, pp. 16-19.

"Yo Ho Ho—Florida's Giveaway Program of Its Sunken Treasure." *Nation,* December 1966, p. 629.

Sources of Information

The following aids are available from the Superintendent of Documents, U.S. Government Printing Office, Washington, D.C. 20402:

A Descriptive List of Treasure Maps and Charts in the Library of Congress (Library of Congress Catalog Card No. 64-60033). Price: $.30

Maps showing explorers' routes, trails, and early roads in the United States, compiled by Richard S. Ladd (Library of Congress Catalog Card No. 62-60066). Price: $1.25

Bulletin, *Hunting for Facts* (U.S. Government Publication No. GP 3.22:F11/963). Price: $.25

A reference service report of available shipwreck data can be obtained from General Services Administration, Archives and Records Service, Washington, D.C. 20408. A bulletin, *Sources of Information Regarding Wrecks in the Great Lakes,* is available from U.S. Army Engineer District, Lake Survey, Corps of Engineers, 630 Federal Building, Detroit, Mich. 48226.

U.S. Geological Survey maps are available from Map Information Service, U.S. Geological Survey, Washington, D.C. 20242. Those who live west of the Mississippi should request maps and information from U.S. Geological Survey, Federal Center, Denver, Colorado 80225. (Either of these offices will send a free map index of any state requested. The information on this index is necessary for ordering of maps.)

Treasure Maps Legend

1. Washington — Gold ingots in barrel buried on Fort Columbia Military Reservation.

2. Oregon — Unknown amount of gold and silver buried in large chest on seaward slope of Neahkahnie Mountain near Nehalem, Tillamook County. Treasure hidden here c. 1679 by survivors of wrecked Spanish galleon. Rocks in area may have cryptic directions to treasure site.

3. Idaho — Bandit loot buried six miles east of Boise on north bank of Boise River.

4. Colorado — Gold bars hidden by early French mining expedition. Location: southeastern Mineral County-Treasure Mountain area.

5. South Dakota — Gold coins, Indian raid loot buried on east bank of Long Lake, east of Lake City, Marshall County.

6. Iowa — Gold dust and nuggets buried in stone jugs by homecoming prospectors, approximately two miles north of Eddyville, Mahaska County.

7. Wyoming — Bandit loot in gold. Buried in Goshen County near old Fort Laramie. Probably close to site of 1880 stagecoach route.

8. North Dakota — Gold dust and nuggets buried for safekeeping on Missouri River at Knife River or Burnt Creek.

9. Michigan — Miscellaneous loot taken by boat from Chicago during 1871 fire. Buried on desolate Cat Head Point.

10. Ontario — Luxury yacht *Gunilda* sunk after hitting "Bread Rock" at Rossport. Loaded with rare antiques and silver, rare wines.

11. Michigan — Steamer *Westmoreland* lost within sight of Sleeping Bear Dune. Large amount of gold reported in captain's safe.

12. Ohio — Valuable relics in shallow water from 1764 Bradstreet and 1763 Wilkins disasters, off Clifton Park, Rocky River, Ohio.

13. Ohio — Steamer *Dean Richmond* sunk in 1893 with $141,000 in gold.

14. Pennsylvania — Huge quantity of silver bars buried in McKean County near Silvermine Run. Hidden by British to prevent capture by Americans at start of 1812 War.

Treasure Maps Legend

15. Tennessee	Large quantity of Civil War treasure reported to be buried a short distance west of Chattanooga.
16. New York State	Captain Kidd's pirate loot. Unknown quantity on Gardiners Island off eastern end of Long Island.
17. Massachusetts	Captain John Quelch's pirate loot, a great quantity of gold and silver coin and bullion. Reported to be buried on Snake Island near Cape Ann.
18. Maine	Pirate hoard buried by Samuel Bellamy near the mouth of the Machias River, Washington County.
19. Nova Scotia	Mystery treasure of Oak Island. Borings have brought up pieces of parchment, coin, and rings.
20. Massachusetts	Pirate Samuel Bellamy lost his ship *Whidah*. Vessel heavily burdened with loot taken from Spanish.
21. Rhode Island	Wreck of German World War II submarine U-853, reported to be carrying $1 million in jewels and U.S. currency.
22. Connecticut	U.S. privateer *Defence*, wrecked on Bartlett's Reef off Waterford, carrying loot from captured British vessels.
23. New York City	H.M.S. *Hussar* sank in the East River in 1780. British gold, payroll on board.
24. North Carolina	S.S. *Central America* lost here in 1857. Over $3 million in gold aboard.
25. Georgia	Gold buried on Blackbeard's Island by pirate captain Blackbeard. Site marked by chain-wrapped tree. If tree is still alive, chain will be overgrown. Put your metal detector to use.
26. Georgia	Confederate Army payroll buried near Kingsland.
27. Florida	Amelia Island gold buried here by pirates and privateer. Some found already.
28. Florida	Gasparilla Island. Gasparilla's flagship sunk by American navy ship. The entire hoard of treasure accumulated by this "king of pirates" was on board the ship when it sank.
29. Florida	Fourteen gold-laden Spanish galleons lost at Long Key in 1715.
30. Florida	Key West. Gold buried by much-feared pirate Black Caesar.
31. Florida	Buried pirate gold worth $15 million near Fowler's Bluff on the Suwannee River. Site is 15 miles upstream from the river mouth, close to village of Chiefland.

32. Ohio	Ohio-Kentucky border around Covington and Cincinnati. Millions of dollars in prohibition bootlegging profits reported to be hidden in the hills within sight of these cities.
33. Tennessee	Buried loot from Civil War action—huge quantity of gold and silver coin, jewelry, and other war loot. Location: close to Owl Creek, northeast of Lexington, Henderson County.
34. Illinois	Cave-In-Rock hideout for many bandits. Bandit loot reported hidden in the area.
35. Arkansas	A hoard of treasure collected by Hernando de Soto is reported to be hidden near Arkadelphia somewhere along the Ouachita River.
36. Texas	Padre Island. Treasure hoards on both private and state land. Treasure hunters here are subject to restrictions of Antiquities Act of 1906.
37. Texas	Gold and jewels buried by pirate captain Jean Lafitte. Buried in a salt flat east of the Lavaca River from the site of Lafitte's sunken flagship, *Pride*.
38. Texas	Lost San Saba mine. Silver bullion hidden in a sealed mine, worth possibly as much as $30 million dollars. Silver originally mined by Spanish. Taken over by Comanche Indians, and later hidden by them. Look northwest of the San Saba River-Silver Creek junction near Menard, Menard County.
39. New Mexico	Hidden gold nuggets in a lost canyon. Gold is hidden in a vault below what was once the stone fireplace of a cabin. Search for this treasure along the Continental Divide on the border of McKinley and Valencia counties.
40. Arizona	Buried cache of gold dust mined by survivors of wrecked Spanish ship *Isabella Catolica*. The search area is from the Mexican border to the Cobabi Mountains.
41. Utah	Incredible treasure of Montezuma is believed buried beneath White Mountain, Johnson's Canyon, approximately 30 miles from Kanab, Kane County.
42. California	Several Spanish galleons lie in vicinity of Santa Catalina Island. One, *Nuestra Señora de Ayuda*, sank here with a $500,000 cargo.
43. California	S.S. *Rio de Janeiro* sank in 1901 off San Francisco with $40,000 in gold aboard plus unknown amount of silver.
44. California	S.S. *R. J. Cochrane* sank in San Francisco Bay in 1911, with close to $100,000 aboard.

Treasure Maps Legend

45. California	Buried gold from 1851 tax collection of Mariposa County. Best location bet is somewhere close to the original county seat of Aqua Fria.
46. California	Wrecked Spanish galleon *San Agustin*. Half-million-dollar precious metal cargo lost on reef of Point Reyes.
47. California	Sidewheel steamer *Brother Jonathan* in 1865 sank off Crescent City. Half-million in gold went down with the ship.
48. California	On Trinity Mountain, close to abandoned mule train trail on Humboldt-Trinity county line, lies hidden bandit loot, $40,000 in gold.
49. Idaho	A wagonload of gold ore possibly hidden in a cave close to the border of Butte and Bingham Counties. Probably within sight of Highway 26.
50. Oregon	Three mystery galleon wrecks in this area. Legends together with artifacts collected in the area support the belief that considerable treasure lies both on shore and in shallow water in the vicinity of the Nehalem River mouth.

Index

Abandoned buildings, searching, 130-131, 135
Agates, 149, 150, 161
Air lift dredge, *see* Dredge
Alabama, Civil War treasure site in, 43
Allied Radio Shack, 171
Americana, buyers of, 40
Antiquities Act, 54, 55
Apostle Islands, 44
Ariel, 68
Arizona:
    ghost towns, 34
    State University, 146
    treasure, 57, 184
Arkansas:
    diamonds, 149
    treasure, 184
Armadas, Spanish, 60
Artifacts, 28, 30, 32, 40, 41
Association, The, 172

Atlantic Coast, 47
Atlases, 26
Avoiding litigation, 165

Ballinger, Gene, 132
Banks:
    officers, 21
    posthole, 39-40
    savings, 21
Bargains in metal-detecting equipment, 90
Batteries, 117
Beaches, 133
Beaver, 68
Beginners, 49
Bellamy, Samuel, 51
Blackbeard, *see* Teach, Captain Edward
Black Hoof, Chief, 28
Bonds treasure site, 52, 53
Books, special collections, 23

Index

Bootleggers' still sites, searching, 138
Boots, 125
Booty, 41
Bottle caps, 31
Bradstreet, Colonel John, 68, 69
Brain power, 22, 25, 71
British Columbia, gold-bearing rivers in, 154-155
Buccaneers, 45-49, 51
Buffington Island, 43. *Also see* Morgan's raid.
Bullion, 58
Burstein-Applebee, 171

Caches, 28, 30
    outlaw, 33
California:
    ghost towns, 34, 35
    gold, 151, 152, 153, 154, 158
    treasure, 184-185
Campsites, 33, 41
Canada, 154
Cannon, 68, 87
Cannonballs, 87
Cape Canaveral, *see* Cape Kennedy
Cape Henlopen, 51
Cape Kennedy, 62
Caribbean, 63, 64
Catalogs of electronic parts supply houses, 171
Cave-in-Rock, 36
Celeron, Pierre Joseph, 15
Centrifugal pump, 155, 158
Chillicothe, 28
Circuit board, printed:
    assembly, 102
    cleaning, 101
    etching, 101
    layout, 99
Circus grounds, 132
Civil War, 41-44, 55
Clark, George Rogers, 28

Cleaning coins, *see* Coins
Clothing for treasure hunting, 125
Coins, 31, 63, 66, 158
    cleaning, 129, 136, 137
    concentrations, 18
    corrosion, 119, 136
    depth under soil, 129
    dimes, 140-141
    dollars, 140-141
    for collectors, 142
    grades, 138
    hot spots, 132
    mint marks, 138-139
    nickels, 140-141
    pennies, 140-141
    selling, 129
    silver in, 143
    value, 139, 140, 141, 143
Coin World, 143
Colorado:
    ghost towns, 34, 35
    gold, 154
    treasure, 182
Compass, 126
Concepcion, 61
Concession stands, 134
Connecticut treasure, 183
Conquistadores, 60
Copper, 38, 161
Corrosion of coins, *see* Coins
Crowds, avoiding, 126

de Braak, 51
Delaware, money beach in, 51-52
Detectors, metal, *see* Metal detectors
Devil's Elbow, 55
Diamonds, prospecting for, 148-149
Diaries, 23
Digging equipment, 121, 167
Dip needles, 73
Disappearing silver coins, 143, 144
Divining pendulum, 71-72, 73-75
Divining rod, 73

Dowsing, 73
Dredge, 155-158
    home-built, 155-157
    operation of, 157-158
D-Tex Electronics, 170
Dumps, farm, 40

East River, Revolutionary War treasure in, 23
Eckert, Allan W., 29
Embezzlement, 25
Empty houses:
    getting permission to search, 163
    treasure hot spots in, 131, 135
Equipment, treasure-hunting, *see* Tools for treasure hunting

Fairgrounds, 132
Faithful Steward, 51
Far West, 32
Filibusters, *see* Buccaneers
Firearms, historic, 14-15
Fisher Research Laboratory, 170
Flea markets, 40
Fleming, Bob, 22
Florida treasure, 60-62, 183
Fly, Captain William, 49
Fort Gibson, 17
Forts, 32
Forty-niners, 155
Free samples of periodicals, 12

Galleons, *see* Spanish galleons, sinking of
Gardiner Electronics Company, 170
Gardiners Island, Captain Kidd's treasure on, 183
Garrett Electronics, 170
Gems, prospecting for, 148-150

Georgia, 57
    buried Confederate Army payroll in, 43, 183
    gold-bearing streams in, 154, 158-159
Ghost towns, 25, 26, 29-30, 32, 34-35
Girona, 59
Gold, 22, 26, 37, 45, 46, 47, 58, 61, 63, 66, 72, 76, 81, 84, 150, 151, 154, 155, 158, 159, 161. *Also see* Bullion.
    bars, 14
    panning, 158, 159, 160
    pirate, 22, 45
    Spanish, 22
Goldak Company, The, 170
Gold Bug, The, 172
Great Lakes, shipwrecks in, 64-70
Griffin, 70
Guadalupe, 64
Gunilda, 182

Handball courts, 133
Heath Company, 170
Hermit Island, treasure of, 44
Hispaniola, 63
Historical societies, 23
History books, 23
Hoarding, 32
Home-built metal detector, 91-114
    case layout, 103
    circuit board, 99
    construction methods, 92
    drilling, 101
    earphones, 104, 105
    electronic parts, 94, 95, 96, 97
    etching, 101
    hardware, 97, 98, 106, 107, 108, 109
    interconnections, 102
    search loop, 109, 110, 111, 112
    soldering, 98, 99, 102
    supplies, 93, 94
    tools, 93

Index

troubleshooting, 114
tryout, 113
Hot spots:
   for coins, 129-135
   in abandoned buildings, 130-131

Idaho:
   gems, 149
   ghost towns, 34
   gold, 154
   opals, 149
   treasure, 182, 185
Illinois, treasure in, *see* Cave-in-Rock
Income tax, 166
Indians, 44, 68-69
   Carib, 45
   history of, 26
   relics of, 54
   silver hoard of the Shawnees, 28-29
   silver mines of, 161
Information, *see* Books, special collections; Maps
Insect repellent, 125
Insurance companies, recovering lost items for, 20
Iowa treasure, 182

Jasper, 149
Johnson, Sir William, 17

Kansas, gold in, 154
Keene dredge, *see* Dredge
Kentucky, Civil War battle site in, 42
Keys, 133-134
Kidd, Captain William, 49

Lafayette Radio Electronics, 171
Lafitte, Jean, buried treasure of, 184
Lake Superior, 44, 150. *Also see* Great Lakes, shipwrecks in.
La Salle, Robert Cavelier, sieur de, 70

Leads, finding, 22-26, 29-30
Le Chameau, 59
Lewis, Captain William, 49
Libraries, 22, 23, 29, 38
Litigation, avoiding, 33
Locators, metal, *see* Metal detectors
Lost-and-found service, operating, 18, 20-21
Lumber camps, abandoned, 135

MacFadden, Bernarr, 38-39
McGee Radio Company, 171
McGinnis, Daniel, 56
Magnetometer, 77, 85-87
Maine, buried treasure in, 183
Maps, 25-26
Massachusetts, treasure sites in, 51, 183
Mercury, sunken, 63-64
Messages, leaving for other treasure hunters, 169
Metal detectors, 7, 18, 20, 26, 29, 44, 127, 143, 145
   batteries, 117
   beat frequency, 29, 77, 78, 79, 80, 81, 84, 85, 87
   depth penetration, 83
   for tone-deaf people, 84
   home building, *see* Home-built metal detector
   induction balance, 77, 81, 83, 84, 85, 87, 88
   manufacturing, 90
   meters, 119
   operating frequency, 80
   prices, 87, 89
   proton magnetometer, 77, 85, 86
   search loop, 80, 81, 109
   transmitter-receiver, 77, 84, 85
   using, 116, 118, 119, 120
Metal locators, *see* Metal detectors

Meteorites:
    payment for finding, 14
    preliminary identification of, 145-147
    submitting for scientific identification, 147-148

Metrotech Underground Explorations, 170

Michigan:
    ghost towns, 32
    lost Indian silver mines in, 161
    treasure, 182

Microfilm, newspapers on, 23, 29

Military relics, 14-15
    from the Civil War, 15, 41-44
    from the French and Indian Wars, 68
    from the War of 1812, 68

Mine detector, 29

Minnesota ghost towns, 32

Mint marks, *see* Coins

Money Island, 49-50

Montana:
    ghost towns, 34, 35
    gold-bearing river in, 154

Moore, Dr. Carleton B., 148

Morgan, General John Hunt, 41

Morgan's raid, 41-43

Mother lode country, 151

National Prospectors Gazette, 172

National Treasure Hunters League, 172

Nebraska, gold-bearing river in, 154

Nevada:
    ghost towns, 34, 35
    gold-bearing rivers in, 154

New Jersey coast, treasures of, 49-50, 52

New Mexico:
    ghost towns, 34, 35
    treasure, 184

Newspapers, 20, 23, 24, 29, 32, 38, 43

New York State, buried pirate treasure in, 183

North Carolina:
    gold-bearing streams in, 154
    rubies and sapphires, 148
    treasure off coast of, 24

North Dakota treasure, 182

Northwest Treasure News, 172

Nova Scotia, 56, 59, 183

Oak Island, treasure of, 56

Occult treasure-finding devices, 71-75

Ohio:
    Indian silver mines in, 161
    lead plates of Pierre Joseph Celeron buried in, 15-16
    route of Morgan's Raid in, 42
    silver hoard of Shawnees in, 28-29
    sunken treasure in Lake Erie, 68-69, 182

Ohio River, 15, 36, 37, 43

Oklahoma, military relics found in, 17

Old Northwest Territory, 15, 17-18, 37

Olson Electronics, 171

Ontario, sunken treasure in, 182

Opals, 149

Oregon:
    agates, 149, 150
    ghost towns, 34, 35
    gold-bearing rivers in, 154
    jasper, 149
    opal, 149
    thunder eggs, 149
    treasure sites in, 182, 185

Outlaw caches, *see* Caches

Padre Island, 54-55

Panning, *see* Gold

Parks, public, 14, 33, 134

Payrolls:
    buried army, 43, 44
    sunken, 59
Pendulum, divining, see Divining pendulum
Pennsylvania treasure, 182
Permission to hunt for treasure, obtaining, 162-163, 164
Permits, for work on Florida wrecks, 62
Pioneer trails, 32-33
Pirates, 37, 45-49, 51, 183, 184
Playgrounds, 132
Pontiac, Chief, 68
Posthole banks, see Banks
Privacy, securing, 126-127
Private property, searching for treasure on, 162-163, 164
Prohibition, 38
Prospecting:
    for gems, 148-150
    for gold, 150-160
    for silver, 161
    for meteorites, 145-148
Prospectors Club International, 172
Proton magnetometer, see Magnetometer
Publicity, shunning, 166

Quartz, gold-bearing, 151
Quebec-Ontario border, gold in streams along, 154
Quinault River, shipwrecks off, 52

Radiesthesia, 72-73
Rayscope Company, 170
Relics, see Military relics
Remick, Ted, 22
Research aids, 22-26
Returning property, 163
Rewards, for finding lost articles, 18, 20

Rhode Island, sunken treasure off, 183
Rings, locating, 18, 19, 20
Rivers, gold-bearing, 152-155
Roberts, Bartholomew, 49
Rocks, identifying as meteorites, 145-147
Rubies, 148

Safety, 125-126
Salvaging, underwater, 58-70
Sapphires, 148
Savings banks, see Banks
Scuba diving, 155
Search and salvage agreements, 163-164
Search oscillator, 79
Semiprecious stones:
    agates, 149, 150
    fairy stones, 150
    opals, 149
    thunder eggs, 149
    topaz, 150
Sharp, Bartholomew, 46
Shawnees, see Indians
Shipwrecks, 50, 51, 58, 59, 60, 61, 62, 65, 66, 181, 182, 183, 184, 185
    souvenirs from, 65
Sifters, 121
Silver:
    coins, disappearance of, 143-144
    Indian mining of, 161
    Shawnee collection of, 28-29
Singer, John, 55
Skin diving, see Scuba diving
Sleeping Bear Sand Dune, 66
Sod:
    removing treasure from, 167, 168
    repairing, 167
Soil removal from coins, see Coins
South Dakota:
    gold-bearing streams in, 154
    treasure site in, 182

Index

Spanish armada of 1588, 59
Spanish galleons, sinking of, 59, 60-62, 63-64
Specie, 47
Stills, *see* Bootleggers' still sites, searching
Storm, Alex, 59
Swings, looking under for coins, 133

Teach, Captain Edward, 48, 49
Tebbs Bend, 42
Tennessee, buried Civil War loot in, 43-44, 183, 184
Texas, treasure sites in, 54-55, 184
Three Brothers, 51
Thunder eggs, 149
Tierra del Fuego, 46
Tolosa, 64
Tools for treasure hunting:
 bag, 122
 basket, 121
 floating sieve, 123-124
 probe, 121, 123
 screen, 122
 shovel, 121
 sifter, 121
Traders, Indian, 26
Trails, pioneer, 32-33
Transistors, 76
Treasure:
 buried, 28-29, 30-32, 32-33, 36, 38-40, 41, 43-44, 47, 49, 55, 56, 129, 134-135
 from shipwrecks, 50-54, 58-70
 Indian, 26, 28-29, 30-32, 161
 outlaw caches, 33, 36-37
 pirate, 47, 49-50, 51
Treasure Hunter, The, 172
Treasure hunters, professional, 11, 22, 126, 132, 166

Treasure News, 172
Treasury Department, 14
Troubleshooting, 114
True Treasure, 172
Trust funds, 23

Underwater prospecting, 155-158
U.S. Geological Survey, maps available from, 25, 181
U.S. Government Printing Office, aids available from, 181
Utah:
 gems, 150
 treasure, 184

Vandalism, avoiding, 166-169
Virginia, fairy stones in, 150
Volleyball courts, 133
Volstead Act, 37

War relics, *see* Military relics
Warships, private, 46-47
Washington:
 ghost towns, 34, 35
 gold, 154
 treasure, 52-53, 182
Western Treasures, 172
Westmoreland, 65
Where to hunt, *see* Treasure
Whidah, 51
White's Electronics, 81, 170
Wilberforce University, 161
Wilkins, Major, 68
Winfield Scott, 59
Wisconsin ghost towns, 32
Wrecks, *see* Shipwrecks
Wyoming:
 ghost towns, 34, 35
 gold, 154
 treasure, 182